Great Depression

Worldwide Economic Depression
That Began in the United States

*(How to Prosper in the Crash Following the
Greatest Boom in History)*

Chad Henry

Published By **Chris David**

Chad Henry

All Rights Reserved

Great Depression: Worldwide Economic Depression That Began in the United States (How to Prosper in the Crash Following the Greatest Boom in History)

ISBN 978-1-7753142-5-7

No part of this guidebook shall be reproduced in any form without permission in writing from the publisher except in the case of brief quotations embodied in critical articles or reviews.

Legal & Disclaimer

The information contained in this book is not designed to replace or take the place of any form of medicine or professional medical advice. The information in this book has been provided for educational & entertainment purposes only.

The information contained in this book has been compiled from sources deemed reliable, and it is accurate to the best of the Author's knowledge; however, the Author cannot guarantee its accuracy and validity and cannot be held liable for any errors or omissions. Changes are periodically made to this book. You must consult your doctor or get professional medical advice before using any of the suggested remedies, techniques, or information in this book.

Upon using the information contained in this book, you agree to hold harmless the Author from and against any damages, costs, and expenses, including any legal fees potentially resulting from the application of any of the information provided by this guide. This disclaimer applies to any damages or injury caused by the use and application, whether directly or indirectly, of any advice or information presented, whether for breach of contract, tort, negligence, personal injury, criminal intent, or under any other cause of action.

You agree to accept all risks of using the information presented inside this book. You need to consult a professional medical practitioner in order to ensure you are both able and healthy enough to participate in this program.

Table Of Contents

Chapter 1: Causes Of The Great Depression 1

Chapter 2: Herbert Hoover 13

Chapter 3: The First One Hundred Days . 27

Chapter 4: The Civilian Conservation Corps 37

Chapter 5: The Federal Music Project 47

Chapter 6: Movies Inside The Nineteen Thirties.. 57

Chapter 7: The Dust Bowl 71

Chapter 8: Dust Pneumonia & Dust Storm Preparations 77

Chapter 9: The Kingfish 95

Chapter 10: Alfalfa Bill Murray 105

Chapter 11: Margaret Mitchell & Gone With The Wind 111

Chapter 12: Dorothea Lange 121

Chapter 13: When It All Came Crashing Down 131

Chapter 14: Hoover Fails And Roosevelt Takes Over 138

Chapter 15: Getting Americans Back To Work 149

Chapter 16: Utilizing A Bit Of American Ingenuity And Knowhow 154

Chapter 17: The Dirty 1930s: Fighting Back Against The Dust Bowl 162

Chapter 18: The Great Depression And The Rise Of Organized Crime 166

Chapter 19: The Lead-As Tons As World War Ii 174

Chapter 1: Causes Of The Great Depression

The Thirties noticed a extended period of economic problems known as the Great Depression. What brought about the Great Depression? Could it have been avoided?

In the Twenties, the united states changed into turning into the arena's principal economic kingdom. The European countries were devastated via the usage of World War I, and America have end up prospering. The advent of strength to American houses had revolutionized ordinary existence. Electric washing machines, vacuum cleaners, irons, radios, and refrigerators were all in excessive name for.

Increased advertising and advertising on radio, and in magazines, handiest reinforced this choice for modern gadgets. Advertisers were stressing to the American humans that they is probably the very last own family on the block to have the cutting-edge day, exceptional product. Americans determined themselves trying devices that, only a few years earlier than, did not even exist.

Unfortunately for clients, quite a few the ones devices have been too steeply-priced for the commonplace character to shop for. A own family might also additionally ought to maintain for years to purchase a bathing machine or an car. This delivered on the development of installment searching out, or purchasing for on credit score rating score. A client would possibly purchase an object by using manner of way of making a small down rate and pay off the relaxation of the price in month-to-month installments. This allowed households to very own gadgets that they will handiest dream of otherwise.

Consumers weren't the high-quality ones looking for on installment. This equal approach of buying come to be getting used in the inventory marketplace. Investors may need to buy shares from a supplier, paying as low as 10% of the inventory's price. As prolonged because the stock fee persevered to upward push, they will pay off the steadiness with little trouble. The stock itself could probable characteristic collateral, which means if the stock price fell, they might lose the stock and nonetheless have to pay off the loan. This approach of purchasing stocks come to be known as searching for on margin.

In the Nineteen Twenties, increasingly more people were turning to the stock marketplace as a method of creating speedy earnings. By 1929, it changed into estimated that about four million Americans were invested inside the inventory marketplace. Many of those inexperienced traders were additionally appealing speculation. This intended they were gambling financially with excessive threat stocks. If the shares have become a achievement, it meant brief earnings. However, speculating on shares, mixed with purchasing for the ones stocks on margin, may additionally additionally want to mean monetary doom for clients if the stock marketplace took a turn for the greater intense.

That is exactly what befell in the fall of 1929. In the final week of October, the stock marketplace started to fail. Nervous buyers began out out to promote their stocks abruptly, which intensified the trouble. On October 29, 1929, the inventory market collapsed. This day is remembered as Black Tuesday.

Banks had been crippled through the stock marketplace crash. In all, 641 banks closed via the stop of 1929. More than five,000 could near within the subsequent numerous years. Many banks also can have survived, however with such pretty some ultimate, Americans panicked. They moved quickly to their very own economic organization to withdraw their coins, fearing it changed into approximately to shut down. This is referred to as a "run at the monetary business enterprise". With no cash to perform with, the financial organization become compelled out of commercial enterprise.

This cycle of catastrophe first-rate persisted. Once consumerism slowed, salespeople had been laid off. Many who worked in manufacturing additionally misplaced their jobs or had their hours and pay significantly cut. As the Depression deepened, masses of heaps of these personnel were laid off. With no earnings, the not unusual citizen can also additionally need to now not find the cash for to repay the debts that they'd incurred through searching for on installment. Since no man or woman became repaying their debts, this crippled even more corporations and monetary establishments. The give up give up result modified into masses of hundreds more dropping their jobs.

Black Tuesday

Most people mark the begin of the Great Depression with a day referred to as Black Tuesday. What happened on Black Tuesday? Why is that day so crucial?

A employer is a industrial business enterprise which individuals purchase inventory in. The extra inventory one owns, the bigger percentage of the enterprise organisation that individual has. These shares are offered, bought, and traded on the inventory trade (the American Stock Exchange is located on Wall Street in New York City). The achievement and failure of these organizations is gauged via using The Dow Jones Industrial Average. The Dow Jones is an index which suggests how big groups are acting at the stock change. If the Dow Jones not unusual is going up, this means that companies are wealthy, and their shareholders are being profitable. If the Dow Jones not unusual is going down, which means that that that a number of the businesses are going through economic hardships.

Throughout the 1920s, the Dow Jones Industrial Average had progressively lengthy beyond up, along facet the remarkable monetary increase in the United States. In fact, it had persisted to rise for nine years in a row. However, in 1929, the stock marketplace located primary fluctuations. Throughout the yr, there were u.S. Of americaand downs as customers bought and supplied in sporadic fashion. During the summer season months, a few monetary analysts predicted a excellent droop, however most did no longer heed this warning.

Thursday, October 24, 1929 modified into the primary day that noticed a dramatic shift. When the inventory exchange on Wall Street opened, there has been heavy buying and selling, with many selecting to promote their shares and get out of the marketplace. This introduced approximately an 11% drop in the fee of the market. A enterprise of predominant bankers even held a meeting to appearance within the event that they is probably able to discover a choice to the panic that had ensued that day.

Monday, October 28, saw even more interest. The Dow Jones Industrial Average spiraled similarly downward. This meant that many shoppers favored to sell their inventory, but no character desired to buy those stocks for the expenses they have been being provided at.

The next day, Tuesday, October 29, 1929, modified into the day on the way to for all time be remembered as Black Tuesday. That day, the Dow Jones Industrial Average fell 30 points, losing 12% of its fee. More than 16 million stocks have been traded, a file that would stand for additonal than 40 years. With such masses of customers searching for to sell off their stocks, hysteria ensued, and loads of human beings misplaced their private fortunes. The inventory market had misplaced greater than $30 billion in cost over the direction of days, and the event became referred to as the Stock Market Crash.

The inventory market persevered to fall even lower over the following weeks in advance than sooner or later stabilizing in mid-November. June of 1930 observed each special hunch inside the marketplace, and however some different downward spiral came about in April of 1931.

Investors had out of region religion inside the American economic device. The decline in stock charges brought approximately financial ruin and employer closures for masses businesses. Expansion and innovation have come to be extra hard as no person desired to make investments their economic capital and take risks. As a stop end result, it'd take extra than a decade for the united states monetary system to get higher. This is why Black Tuesday is considered the occasion that commenced the Great Depression.

Hoovervilles & The Bonus Army

During the years of the Great Depression, Hoovervilles sprang up throughout America. What became a Hooverville? Why modified into it called that?

As the Great Depression persisted to worsen, many that had misplaced their jobs have been compelled to depart their homes. With no place to live, those human beings, or maybe whole families, have been forced to locate secure haven anywhere they could. In many times, the handiest preference modified into for the homeless to assemble shacks, or shanties, constituted of whatever and the whole lot they'll locate. Boxes, wooden crates, tar-paper, or maybe vintage sheets have been being applied as makeshift homes.

Villages of these shacks sprang up in parks and empty plots of land at some level within the united states of america. Many cities should not allow the homeless to congregate on this manner, so the shacks ought to display up on the outskirts of city, or simply outside town limits. The time period "shantytown" have turn out to be quite not unusual to present an cause of the ones types of dwellings. However, due to the fact such numerous inside the nation saw President Herbert Hoover as being responsible for the economic woes, a today's call emerged. Many humans started out calling the villages "Hoovervilles".

In 1932, a disgruntled organization of homeless World War I veterans determined to create a Hooverville in Washington DC. They positioned their little network at the National Mall, in most of the Washington and Lincoln monuments. Another Hooverville turned into installation surely at some point of the Potomac River, where it can be visible with the aid of these in Washington D.C. Between the 2 places, greater than 15,000 veterans, their better halves, and youngsters had collected together.

Their purpose changed into to protest Congress and the president, stressful that they get maintain of coins they felt have end up owed to them. In 1924, the World War Adjustment Act were passed. This regulation stated that each one veterans will be paid an advantage to make up for the wages they will were making sooner or later of the conflict. Unfortunately, this cash changed into now not speculated to be paid until 1944. In the midst of the financial hardships they have been going through, those veterans insisted that the coins be paid faster, in preference to later. They cited themselves due to the fact the Bonus Expeditionary Force.

The B.E.F. Became informed through the government to disperse and flow decrease again to their homes. However, quite some them didn't have a home to move returned to. Nearly 2,000 individuals of this "Bonus Army" refused to go away. President Hoover ordered General Douglas MacArthur to cast off them from the city. Using tear gas and rifles, troops rapid cleared the National Mall earlier than crossing the Potomac to move on the second camp. The usa grow to be in marvel. American squaddies had attacked homeless veterans, setting fireside to their shacks and huts.

Chapter 2: Herbert Hoover

Herbert Hoover is visible with the aid of using some because of the truth the president liable for the Great Depression. Who have come to be Herbert Hoover? Did he take any efforts to remedy the monetary problems the dominion changed into handling?

Born in Iowa, in 1874, Herbert Hoover modified into the son of a blacksmith. He attended Stanford in 1891 and graduated 4 years later with a degree in Geology. Hoover made his financial fortune as a mining engineer. He revamped $4 million mining for silver, lead, and zinc.

The direction of his lifestyles changed sooner or later of World War I, despite the fact that. As the battle started out out, he orchestrated an evacuation of Americans who've been looking for to get out of Europe and return home. He and 500 volunteers worked to distribute steamship tickets, garb, and food to more than 100 twenty,000 people. Hoover additionally undertook a comfort try to offer meals for the country of Belgium, which modified into struggling after the German invasion.

In 1917, President Woodrow Wilson named Hoover due to the fact the top of the U.S. Food Administration. In this feature, he organized wartime rationing efforts which include "Meatless Mondays" and "Wheatless Wednesdays". When the warfare concluded, he shipped big quantities of food to the ravenous people of crucial Europe, even to the defeated u . S . A . Of Germany. He moreover sent food to the residents of Bolshevik-controlled Russia. As the ultimate decade came to an give up, The New York Times named Herbert Hoover among their "Ten Most Important Living Americans".

After Warren Harding modified into elected president in 1920, he appointed Hoover to the location of Secretary of Commerce. Hoover grew to emerge as the place of business into an critical characteristic, encouraging "financial modernization" and overseeing the whole thing from air tour to the census. He furthermore began an "non-public your house" advertising campaign, which spurred domestic creation. He is regularly appeared due to the reality the top notch Secretary of Commerce in U.S. Records.

In 1928 he have turn out to be the 31st President of the us. This made him one in every of excellent presidents who had by no means held a previous elected office or excessive military rank. He had simplest been president for 8 months at the equal time as the stock marketplace crashed in 1929, which, of direction, precipitated the Great Depression.

He is frequently criticized for doing little to try to combat the Great Depression. At that point, america had a laissez-faire method to monetary subjects. This intended that the government did now not intervene with financial topics and clearly left the economic device on my own. However, Hoover began out severa public works duties, at the side of the Hoover Dam, and raised the exquisite tax bracket from 25% to 63%. He additionally installed the Reconstruction Finance Corporation, which loaned $238 million to banks and railroad organizations. Many of the measures Hoover took were just like efforts Franklin Roosevelt may need to later make.

Despite those efforts, via 1932, unemployment have grow to be over 24%, extra than five,000 banks had failed, and tens of masses of Americans have been homeless. The shantytowns that they developed have become known as Hoovervilles, in honor of the president they noticed as answerable for their scenario.

While Hoover is still considered via using a few as "the president who brought about the Great Depression", his recognition has improved notably over time. He have turn out to be the closing president to hold a complete cabinet position previous to being elected, and he moreover laid hundreds of the foundation for the New Deal applications of the Nineteen Thirties.

Franklin D. Roosevelt

The president who oversaw maximum of the Thirties modified into Franklin Roosevelt. What did Franklin Roosevelt accomplish as president? Why have grow to be he so well-known?

Franklin Roosevelt became born in Hyde Park, New York in 1882. His mother and father have been every from wealthy families, and greater youthful Franklin lived a privileged lifestyles. He became a mean pupil in university, however attended Harvard and graduated with a degree in History.

In 1921, Roosevelt contracted polio. As a end end result, he have turn out to be completely paralyzed from the waist down. In private, he used a wheelchair, however took first rate lengths to cowl his incapacity from the general public. Even on the same time as he changed into president, most Americans did now not comprehend he changed into not able to walk.

He first made a name for himself in authorities due to the fact the Assistant Secretary of the Navy. He then went without delay to be elected governor of New York in 1928 (and once more in 1930). In 1932, the USA become in the midst of the Great Depression, and Franklin Roosevelt ran for president. He ran on the promise of a "new deal" for the American people and obtained all but 6 states.

His New Deal applications drastically altered the arrival of the country. Programs which includes the WPA, CCC, and TVA positioned lots of humans to paintings and helped create the infrastructure of the dominion. The WPA built roads, bridges, dams, lakes, and storm drainage sewers. The CCC progressed parks, built lakes, planted timber, and created terraces to help combat wind erosion, whilst the TVA built more than 40 dams in seven Southern states. This averted flooding inside the region and installation electric powered strength grids to run off of hydroelectricity.

Roosevelt extended the dimensions and scope of presidency quite. His management created dozens of recent government businesses that assumed many great obligations. During his presidency, great exertions legal guidelines (which incorporates minimum income and a forty four hour paintings week) were moreover handed, exertions unions were reinforced, and the authorities have turn out to be a tool to steer and govern the monetary device.

As the 1930s have become the 1940s, Franklin Roosevelt persisted serving as president throughout World War II. His control and desire-making capability helped the usa navigate via the war years and turn out to be the dominant military strength in the global.

Franklin Roosevelt is the simplest president to serve extra than two terms in workplace. He grow to be elected to the location four times (1932, 1936, 1940, and 1944). This had a dramatic impact at america of a and brought about the passage of the twenty second Amendment to the US Constitution. This trade states that no president can also moreover serve extra than phrases.

Roosevelt became not with out his critics. Many of his warring parties disliked the New Deal, claiming he become primary America down the path of socialism. He became moreover criticized closely for his try to percentage the Supreme Court with justices favorable to his pointers. After Congress and the court docket tool commenced tough or rejecting hundreds of his New Deal applications, he attempted to increase the range of Supreme Court justices from 9 to fifteen. This would have allowed him to lease all six of the modern-day justices and stability the Court in his want.

Despite the ones criticisms, Roosevelt modified into very famous in the direction of his presidency and remains so in recent times. There is a monument in Washington DC devoted in his honor. His image appears on the dime, and there are various parks, schools, and different homes named after him. He is frequently indexed the diverse maximum influential presidents the us has ever had.

Franklin Roosevelt's

1933 Inaugural Address

March 4, 1933

I am sure that my fellow Americans assume that on my induction into the Presidency I will deal with them with a candor and a choice which the present state of affairs of our humans impel. This is preeminently the time to speak the reality, the entire reality, frankly and boldly. Nor want we reduce from simply going through conditions in our u.S.A. These days. This splendid Nation will undergo because it has persevered, will revive and will prosper. So, first of all, permit me assert my corporation perception that the only difficulty we need to fear is worry itself—anonymous, unreasoning, unjustified terror which paralyzes favored efforts to convert retreat into boom. In each dark hour of our countrywide lifestyles a management of frankness and power has met with that knowledge and manual of the people themselves this is crucial to victory. I am glad that you may once more deliver that help to management in these critical days.

In this sort of spirit on my factor and on yours we're handling our not unusual issues. They task, thank God, best material matters. Values have shrunken to first-rate stages; taxes have risen; our ability to pay has fallen; government of a sizeable range is confronted via the use of critical curtailment of profits; the way of alternate are frozen inside the currents of trade; the withered leaves of industrial commercial company enterprise lie on every thing; farmers find no markets for his or her produce; the savings of many years in hundreds of families are lengthy lengthy long gone.

More vital, a number of unemployed residents face the lousy trouble of lifestyles, and an in addition wonderful range toil with little go back. Only a silly optimist can deny the dark realities of the instant…

… Restoration calls, however, no longer for adjustments in ethics by myself. This Nation asks for movement, and movement now. Our outstanding primary challenge is to place human beings to artwork. This isn't always any unsolvable hassle if we're managing it as it should be and courageously. It may be completed in element through direct recruiting via the Government itself, treating the mission as we would deal with the emergency of a warfare, but on the same time, via this employment, mission appreciably desired duties to stimulate and reorganize using our herbal belongings…

…If I take a look at the mood of our people efficiently, we now understand as we have in no way found out in advance than our interdependence on each other; that we cannot simply take however we ought to supply as nicely; that if we're to transport in advance, we need to bypass as a educated and regular army willing to sacrifice for the first-rate of a commonplace vicinity, because with out such challenge no development is made, no management will become powerful. We are, I recognize, organized and willing to region up our lives and belongings to such area, because it makes possible a control which targets at a bigger real. This I advocate to offer, pledging that the bigger abilties will bind upon us all as a sacred obligation with a brotherly love of responsibility hitherto evoked first-rate in time of armed strife.

With this pledge taken, I expect unhesitatingly the manage of this great navy of our human beings devoted to a disciplined attack upon our not unusual troubles.

Action on this image and to this stop is possible beneath the shape of presidency which we've inherited from our ancestors. Our Constitution is so smooth and realistic that it is feasible continuously to satisfy awesome needs by changes in emphasis and affiliation without loss of crucial form. That is why our constitutional tool has proved itself the maximum superbly enduring political mechanism the modern-day global has produced. It has met every pressure of big enlargement of territory, of remote places wars, of sour inner strife, of global own family members.

It is to be hoped that the everyday stability of presidency and legislative authority can be very well well sufficient to meet the high-quality challenge earlier than us. But it may be that an tremendous call for and need for undelayed motion can also call for transient departure from that ordinary stability of public manner.

I am prepared beneath my constitutional duty to suggest the measures that a troubled state in the midst of a afflicted global can also moreover furthermore require. These measures, or such other measures as the

Congress can also assemble out of its revel in and expertise, I shall are looking for, inside my constitutional authority, to deliver to speedy adoption.

But within the event that the Congress shall fail to take this type of two guides, and inside the event that the countrywide emergency continues to be critical, I shall now not steer clear of the clear direction of duty with the intention to then confront me. I shall ask the Congress for the simplest closing tool to meet the catastrophe—big Executive strength to profits a conflict in opposition to the emergency, as top notch due to the fact the strength that might get hold of to me if we had been in fact invaded with the aid of way of a overseas foe.

Chapter 3: The First One Hundred Days

Franklin Roosevelt's administration is well-known for carrying out many stuff in its "first hundred days". What did he try this have become so considerable? How did it change the united states?

As Franklin Roosevelt modified into making geared up to go into the White House, he consulted the reviews of severa human beings that he had trusted for years. Adolph Berle, Raymond Moley, and Rexford Tugwell had been professors at Columbia University and guys who had secretly cautioned the president all through his years as governor of New York. These men came to be referred to as the Brain Trust. Roosevelt may additionally regularly propose mind to them and concentrate to their evaluations and recommendation. While the Brain Trust in no manner officially met in the course of his presidency, the trio in reality had have an impact on over his selection-making approach. Roosevelt had awesome close to advisers that he consulted as well, masses of whom have grow to be a part of manipulate. Of direction, his closest advisor turn out to be his spouse Eleanor.

When Roosevelt assumed the presidency in March of 1933, his first movement have become to order all banks to take a vacation for 4 days. By doing this, he was hoping to calm humans's anxieties approximately the banking corporation. Fearful citizens had been attempting to pull their coins out of banks, believing they might close to. This "vacation" gave all of us a risk to lighten up, and banks reopened four days later, with few human beings dashing to take their coins out.

Following that, the brand new president known as a totally specific session of Congress. After Roosevelt had been in place of work for best 4 days, the primary of the New Deal legal tips (the Emergency Banking Relief Act) grow to be passed. This changed into followed thru a slew of law, maximum of which took place from March 20th thru June sixteenth of 1933.

The Economy Act, signed on March 20th, end up designed to balance the federal fee variety thru decreasing government salaries. The Federal Emergency Relief Act legal $500 million to provide remedy for negative households, within the form of food and garb. Other important portions of regulations covered the Agricultural Adjustment Act, the Federal Securities Act, and the National Employment System Act.

During the number one hundred days, Roosevelt furthermore created the Civilian Conservation Corps, which supplied 250,000 jobs for guys among the a while of 18 and 25. The Tennessee Valley Authority have become moreover installed. This task may build hydroelectric dams and provide energy to the Tennessee Valley vicinity.

The "first 100 days" altered the manner that many view the place of work of the president. At the time, many in Washington DC had been important of the brand new president for doing an excessive amount of too fast.

However, nowadays an incoming president is frequently seemed through how lots is, or isn't, finished in the path of the number one hundred days of the administration.

The New Deal

When Franklin Roosevelt have end up president, he furnished a "New Deal" for the American people. What changed into the New Deal? How was it set up region?

One of the primary motives Roosevelt obtained the presidency in 1932 became because of the fact he promised to attempt to do something to give up the economic crisis america come to be going through. As he entered the office, Roosevelt hoped to do three subjects. First, he hoped to provide consolation for the terrible and the unemployed. Next, he wanted the economic device to get higher to its ordinary ranges. Finally, he wanted to reform the economic systems just so an economic melancholy would possibly now not display up all over again. Relief, recuperation, and reform have become called the three R's.

To accomplish these dreams, Roosevelt implemented a sequence of presidency applications in among 1933 and 1938. Some of those programs have been approved by the use of Congress, at the same time as others he enforced via government order. Collectively, the ones programs have become called "The New Deal".

The New Deal is frequently stated in one in all a type additives. The "First New Deal" (1933-1934) emerge as in big component concerned with restructuring the country's economic device and presenting remedy to the banking enterprise. The "Second New Deal" (1935-1938) sought to improve using the u . S .'s property, furnished consolation for farmers, and created various authorities art work packages.

There had been many first-rate styles of packages that had been part of the New Deal. These applications had a number of awesome supposed purposes. Programs which incorporates the Works Progress Administration (WPA) and the Civilian Conservation Corps (CCC) had been designed to location unemployed people to paintings. The Social Security Act come to be created to provide financial relief to the aged. Meanwhile, the Tennessee Valley Authority added plenty desired strength to rural areas inside the South.

The Federal Deposit Insurance Corporation (FDIC) changed into every other important enterprise organization created via the New Deal. The FDIC guaranteed the safety of cash in banks. Citizens not had to fear losing their coins if their monetary group closed (this situation became quite common in the early levels of the Depression). The FDIC remains in operation nowadays to insure cash deposited in banks.

Aside from the FDIC, there are numerous authorities groups that had been created through using the New Deal which although exist. Amongst them are the Federal Housing Administration (FHA), the Federal Crop Insurance Corporation (FCIC), and the Securities Exchange Commission (SEC).

Not everyone modified into eager at the New Deal. Many felt that Roosevelt changed into critical the USA down the direction of socialism. Others observed the New Deal responsibilities as a waste of coins and assets. Today, some economists and historians accept as proper with that Roosevelt's adherence to New Deal suggestions absolutely extended the Great Depression.

However, New Deal applications did positioned masses of lots of human beings to work, imparting economic comfort for suffering households. The New Deal duties furthermore allowed for the development of roads, faculties, parks, hospitals, and lots of distinct facilities that have been preferred ultimately of the state.

The Works Progress Administration

One of the most ambitious applications enacted with the resource of the Franklin Roosevelt Administration in the direction of the Great Depression modified into the Works Progress Administration (WPA). What changed into the WPA? What forms of initiatives were they involved with?

Created thru an government order from President Roosevelt, the cause of the Works Progress Administration turned into to provide a paying technique for any family whose primary salary-earner modified into unemployed. Most of the humans the WPA hired were unskilled people who have been employed for creation obligations.

There had been many unique types of WPA duties. Parks, bridges, roads, courthouses, schools, and hospitals had been all built through WPA personnel. Museums, town halls, and swimming swimming swimming pools had been built as properly. To at the prevailing time, maximum groups in the United States have a park, bridge, or college that end up built by the use of the use of the commercial corporation agency. The software program substantially benefited rural areas within the South and western regions of the country wherein centers on the side of the ones were desperately wanted.

The WPA moreover assisted ladies who located themselves unemployed all through the Great Depression. The Household Service Demonstration Project knowledgeable 30,000 girls in skills needed to be a domestic servant (which includes a housekeeper or maid). Trainees have been taught a manner to cook dinner, sew, wash and iron clothes, and masses of different capabilities that might be wanted.

Not all the WPA packages have been for unskilled employees. The Federal Theatre Project, Federal Writers Project, Federal Music Project, and Federal Art Project have been all branches of the WPA alleged to assist out-of-artwork authors, artists, actors, and musicians.

Not certainly all and sundry accepted of the WPA. Many felt that such authorities work programs were a manner of introducing communism into the usa. Additionally, some believed that WPA creation efforts have been being allotted on a political foundation. For example, they claimed that the South obtained a huge full-size form of WPA projects because of the fact President Roosevelt hoped to win votes in that part of the county. Others felt that WPA employees were lazy and advanced bad paintings behavior at the same time as worried in the application.

Chapter 4: The Civilian Conservation Corps

One of the maximum famous programs implemented with the useful useful resource of Franklin Roosevelt as a part of the New Deal changed into the Civilian Conservation Corps (CCC). What became the CCC? Who end up it supposed for?

The Civilian Conservation Corps have become began in March of 1933 as a piece remedy software program. It become alleged to provide jobs for younger unmarried guys, age 18-25, who had been out of work due to the Great Depression. By July of 1933, there have been 250,000 greater youthful men enrolled, running in 1,463 unique camps.

When one have grow to be a member of the CCC, he signed a dedication to take part within the software program for as a minimum six months. At the perception of this term, he have to select out out to enlist for a few different six months. The most restriction turn out to be a whole of 4 phrases (or years) that one could live in the utility.

Each enlistee became required to take a bodily exam preceding to turning into a member of. Physical fitness modified into critical due to the disturbing difficult artwork that is probably involved.

Each CCC worker turned into given meals, housing, a uniform, and thirty dollars a month. Twenty-5 of the thirty bucks emerge as despatched home to their parents. The personnel lived in camps and have been housed in barracks (fifty people to a tent). Aside from the barracks, the CCC camps additionally featured an schooling constructing, a systematic facility, a massive variety corridor, a organisation location, restrooms and showers, a tool room and blacksmith store, and garages.

The primary characteristic of the CCC changed into to keep herbal assets and smooth up the countrywide parks and forests. Their first actual responsibilities associated with soil erosion manage in Alabama. Soil erosion tasks have end up mainly vital in the Great Plains states, which have been being ravaged with the aid of the usage of using the Dust Bowl. One of the most important CCC duties end up reforestation (planting wooden). The trees were had to characteristic wind blocks, which helped manage the soil erosion problem.

Before lengthy, CCC camps had been anywhere inside the usa, tackling many exceptional forms of responsibilities. CCC duties included the whole thing from constructing fireplace lookout towers, roads, and airport touchdown fields, to controlling insects and sicknesses, fish stocking, and casting off predatory animals. They additionally built terraces, built dams, and installation campgrounds.

By 1940, this system started out being decreased extensively. The Great Depression changed into coming close to its stop, and there was plenty much less want to rent extra younger personnel. In 1941, at the same time as the USA entered World War II, this want have turn out to be even a good buy much less, because of the reality most guys of this age had been each enlisting or being drafted to help in the conflict strive. The software changed into formally ended on June 30, 1942.

At the time of its stop, the CCC had hired over 2.Five million younger guys. They had built over 90 seven,000 miles of avenue, constructed extra than 800 parks, and planted more than three billion bushes.

The Tennessee Valley Authority

During the Thirties, there had been few regions of the usa that have been worse off than the place known as the Tennessee Valley. Where is the Tennessee Valley? How did the New Deal help this place?

The area referred to as the Tennessee Valley includes portions of Tennessee, Alabama, Mississippi, Georgia, and Kentucky. For years, this place become a long manner behind the rest of the country in masses of areas of lifestyles. Electricity, jogging water, sewers, and proper sanitation had been all factors of our current existence which have been sorely lacking in the Tennessee Valley sooner or later of the Thirties. One of the most important desires of many New Deal packages changed into to assist modernize the South and decorate dwelling conditions within the ones states.

The maximum notable of those New Deal applications have become called the Tennessee Valley Authority (TVA). The TVA's purpose became to build hydroelectric dams within the course of the place, that may supply electricity into hundreds of houses. Eventually, the TVA ought to accumulate and hold more than 30 hydroelectric dams that provided less expensive strength to tens of millions of Southerners. In 1933, it grow to be expected that pleasant 2% of houses in the Tennessee Valley had strength. By 1945, this quantity have been improved to seventy five%.

Bringing energy to the region have end up as an alternative essential. Not exceptional did home domestic device and electric powered powered lights make life less complicated, however there have been precise benefits as nicely. Factories and other organizations have been now able to locate within the vicinity and hire thousands of employees.

There had been additionally health benefits to the extended availability of energy. Better lighting intended progressed eyesight and a reduced threat of injuries. Electric fridges allowed Southerners to maintain food longer with out it spoiling. This meant they'll buy meals from the grocery shop, in place of relying on homegrown produce and dairy merchandise.

Electricity additionally supposed that Southerners also can want to purchase what the rest of the united states of america were taking detail in for the beyond decade or greater, a radio. The radio proved very vast in the isolated Tennessee Valley area. It helped

Southerners enjoy more associated with the rest of the u . S .. They have to now be aware of the same facts and radio programs that humans from New York to Los Angeles had been being attentive to.

Aside from supplying electricity, the TVA changed into moreover concerned with soil conservation. The company promoted the use of fertilizers and crop rotation to decorate soil situations. The TVA moreover had applications to decorate fish and flora and fauna habitats, control wild fires, and replant forests.

The TVA modified into not commonly famous. The introduction of the hydroelectric dams introduced about extra than 15,000 households to lose their houses. Those regions have been flooded to make lakes and reservoirs. Also, many Southerners had been suspicious of government officials. Therefore, the TVA needed to recruit close by citizens to speak to their buddies approximately soil conservation strategies.

Other New Deal packages had been created to help fight illnesses. Hookworm, pellagra, malaria, typhoid, and diphtheria had prolonged plagued the South. These ailments were unfold via lousy sewage and sanitation structures (which allowed germs and bacteria to unfold swiftly). New sewer structures in important towns helped reduce the extensive form of deaths due to diphtheria and typhoid. New water treatment facilities moreover progressed the state of affairs of eating water.

Swamp drainage in South Carolina resulted in a sixteen% drop in malaria cases, and mosquito eradication efforts helped reduce malaria-related deaths thru sixty six%. There had been similar successes in decreasing the amount of times of dysentery, hookworm, and pellagra.

Radio in the 1930s

The maximum well-known shape of leisure in the Nineteen Thirties have become radio. What were some of the maximum listened to radio applications? Who had been the biggest radio celebrities of the day?

Radio burst onto the scenes in 1920 and fast have end up a rustic huge craze. No extraordinary new product caught on as rapid as radio. Everyone desired to have one in every of their domestic. Two years after radios went within the marketplace, radio income were bringing in extra than $60 million a twelve months.

Radios got here in all styles and sizes too. The least costly models may be purchased for about $eight. A excellent radio may cost a little about $50. The maximum highly-priced radios to be had on the market have been the dimensions of a chest-of-drawers and fee more than $500! By the dawn of the Thirties, approximately 1/2 of of the houses in the u . S . Had a radio. There were moreover greater than 500 radio stations working in the United States.

Radio networks fast evolved programming to entertain their listeners. During the workday, even as most listeners have been housewives, romance and drama packages have been featured. The Romance of Helen Trent, Stella Dallas, and Life may be Beautiful had been all famous programs. These shows were typically subsidized through merchandise that housewives wanted, which includes laundry cleansing cleaning soap. Thus, those programs have end up known as "cleaning soap operas".

The after college hours were generally entire of movement and adventure applications for kids. Flash Gordon, Hop Harrigan, Sky King, and Superman had been the diverse maximum famous. These applications typically ran 15 mins and saved kids engaged while their mother prepared the middle of the night meal.

Chapter 5: The Federal Music Project

One of the greater exciting New Deal applications have become known as the Federal Music Project. What became the Federal Music Project? How prolonged did it exist?

Many musicians had been harm badly through the usage of the Great Depression. During a time of such financial problem, there were fewer and less people hiring stay musicians or paying to attend live shows. These varieties of performances have been taken into consideration luxuries, which the not unusual circle of relatives should no longer come up with the money for. Additionally, new technological improvements in recording strategies, particularly information and record game enthusiasts, lessened the need for live musicians.

In 1935, the Federal Music Project (FMP) have become created with the aim of using as many out of labor musicians as viable. They can also art work as instrumentalists, singers, and performers, exciting humans across the country. Aside from using the musicians, the mission had distinct goals. First, they hoped to provide a miles wanted distraction for commonplace folks who were suffering thru the financial disaster. Also, they was hoping to supply a better degree of subculture and sophistication to their audiences. Because of the economic hardships, admission to the ones live performance events come to be provided at very much less high-priced expenses, or, frequently free of rate.

The FMP had other obligations as nicely. Aside from unique the hundreds, the FMP moreover meant to teach them. Trained musicians running for the FMP provided track training to adults who could not find the money for non-public commands. It additionally created network orchestras and choirs, similarly to beginning track programs for children. The FMP have grow to be so successful that most colleges in the usa had their non-public track utility.

The final task of the FMP worried discovering, gathering, and retaining America's musical historic past. FMP human beings scoured the usa to document or write down each music they may. Every type of music become catalogued from hillbilly, to jazz, human beings, Creole, gospel, and African American.

Unfortunately, like many of the exceptional New Deal programs, the Federal Music Project's price range became reduced in 1939. That equal yr, the project have emerge as renamed the WPA Music Program. A 12 months later, it come to be terminated all together.

The Federal Music Project lasted first-class 4 years, however it become pretty a fulfillment in that component. FMP musicians done loads of stay shows for heaps and thousands of human beings. There have been furthermore more than 30 orchestras created throughout the country, as well as infinite network developing a song companies. Perhaps most importantly, the song of the country's common humans modified into accrued and preserved for destiny generations.

Big Bands & Swing Music

In the Thirties, many younger Americans began listening to swing music. What changed into swing? Who had been the maximum essential performers?

Big band track emerge as all of the rage within the 1930s. "Big bands" had been jazz or swing bands, typically composed of approximately 12 to twenty-five musicians. The instrumentation generally protected saxophones, trumpets, trombones, clarinets, drums, and a standup bass.

One of the earliest stars of the swing era changed into Duke Ellington. Ellington have turn out to be a composer, pianist, and bandleader who've emerge as well-known inside the past due Twenties. In 1926, he and his corporation have grow to be the residence band at the well-known Cotton Club in New York City. The Cotton Club became an particular region with rich clients. However, every week there was a everyday radio broadcast from the Cotton Club, which gave Ellington countrywide publicity. Ellington remained one of the most well-known figures in track in some unspecified time in the future of the Thirties, generating classics along side "I Got it Bad", "Mood Indigo", and of direction, "It Don't Mean a Thing (If It Ain't Got That Swing)."

Another dominant determine of Thirties swing track emerge as Benny Goodman. In fact, Benny Goodman earned the popularity because the "King of Swing". Goodman changed into a clarinetist and the leader of his very personal swing band. Goodman have grow to be tremendously well-known within the latter half of of the Thirties.

The seminal occasion for 1930s swing tune happened on January 16, 1938. It turn out to be a live average overall performance referred to as Benny Goodman at Carnegie Hall. The King of Swing took the extent alongside side Duke Ellington, Count Basie (each special well-known bandleader), Gene Krupa (a famous drummer), and lots of unique musicians. They done for hours within the the front of a presented-out Carnegie Hall. This concert is regarded via many because the immediate when jazz and swing music received complete popularity via mainstream audiences.

Swing tune moreover produced severa dances. The jitterbug changed into a very famous dance craze at a few level in the 1930s. The Lindy Hop have emerge as moreover very popular inside the past due Nineteen Twenties and early '30s. Swing even produced a whole shape of dance, swing dance, which remains famous today.

Those who followed swing tune carefully even superior their personal slang language. Terms which includes "hipster", "hepcat", and "jive" all have grow to be not unusual. "In the groove" and "jam session" had been famous as nicely. Many of those terms had been introduced to the contemporary-day lexicon and are even though used in recent times.

Swing music is visible as large no longer truly due to the extraordinary tune that changed into produced. It is likewise seemed as important for helping to break down racial barriers. White audiences have been gambling the music of African American performers, and musicians of numerous races were taking the level to perform together.

Today, Duke Ellington, Benny Goodman, and hundreds of diverse swing performers are remembered a number of the greats of American well-known tune. Their song is cherished to these days, and lots of contemporary musicians claim them as musical affects.

War of the Worlds

The "War of the Worlds" broadcast become one of the most memorable sports activities to arise in the 1930s. What happened throughout this broadcast? Who perpetrated this stunt?

On October 30, 1938, the Mercury Theatre Radio Group aired a dramatic radio presentation of the traditional HG Wells novel The War of the Worlds. The novel conveys the story of an alien invasion of Earth. The organization wearing out the published provided the tale in a modern putting and modified the extent to New York and New Jersey (the proper novel occurred in England).

The story have grow to be furnished in real time, as if the events had been surely taking place. Regular tune programming end up periodically interrupted with "unique bulletins" which knowledgeable the listeners of the trendy news regarding the alien invasion. Many humans heard the ones opinions and believed the invasion turned into in reality happening.

At the begin of the posted, there was an declaration declaring that the program come to be a radio drama. Unfortunately, many human beings unnoticed this statement. Thousands of listeners known as the police. Some went outside and glad themselves that they could see flashes of mild inside the distance because of the truth the "struggle" ensued. Others have been extraordinary they'll fragrance toxic gases being fired via the usage of one side or the other.

There had been incidents of hysteria all for the duration of the us of america. Many human beings rushed into the streets with shotguns and rifles, organized to war the unknown alien enemy. Others fled to the hills, attempting to interrupt out the towns.

The state of affairs changed into made more and more worse due to the truth the broadcasters were using real region names. For instance, the preliminary alien landing changed into supposed to have taken region at Grover's Mill. Crowds of people arrived at this area with guns and distinct guns. As a result, the police and fireplace department have been compelled to move there and manipulate the crowds. Bystanders who noticed the mass of armed residents, police, and firemen had no desire however to accept as true with that the rumors of alien invasion were actual.

Chapter 6: Movies Inside The Nineteen Thirties

Movies have been becoming a number one part of normal existence in America inside the route of the Nineteen Thirties. Who had been the most famous movie stars of the technology? What did the movies imply to the people in that decade?

In 1927, a film titled The Jazz Singer debuted. This have turn out to be the number one film to characteristic sound (all movies prior to that have been silent movies). Ever because of the fact that that factor, the movie company has been a booming business inside the United States. Even inside the Nineteen Thirties, in some unspecified time in the future of the Great Depression, 80 million movie tickets had been provided every week.

There have been many massive-call stars for the duration of the remaining decade collectively with Errol Flynn, James Cagney, and Edward G. Robinson. Cagney and Robinson have been satisfactory recognized for his or her roles in gangster films like The Hatchet Man (Robinson) or G-Men (Cagney). America have become considering more youthful actors and actresses like Mickey Rooney, Judy Garland, and of direction, "America's little darling" Shirley Temple.

The biggest film celebrity of the final decade have emerge as Clark Gable. From 1930 to 1939, he made thirty-9 films. He portrayed many one-of-a-kind styles of characters, from a cowboy, to a gangster, reporter, chauffer, gambler, legal professional, medical doctor, minister, and miner. However, he is going to generally be brilliant remembered for his function as Rhett Butler within the 1939 film Gone with the Wind.

Gone with the Wind stays one of the maximum famous and maximum severely acclaimed movies of all time. It grossed nearly $ hundred million in theaters. This made it the most financially a hit movie ever made, a file it held for 26 years. When adjusted for inflation, it remains the most a fulfillment movie of all time.

1939 is frequently seemed because the quality 12 months in cinematic history. Aside from Gone with the Wind, severa exceptional tremendous films were launched that twelve months. Wuthering Heights (starring Laurence Olivier), Mr. Smith Goes to Washington (supplying Jimmy Stewart), Stage Coach (with John Wayne), and The Wizard of Oz are nevertheless appeared as classics these days.

Movie theaters of the Thirties were grand, stylish structures. Many theaters had chandeliers or one of a kind pricey capabilities inside the foyer. The seats in each theater were best and lush, and the display show became inside the back of an ornate curtain that opened at the same time as the film began out.

Each movie commenced out with a newsreel, previews of coming factors of interest, and a cool lively film. These lively shorts brought moviegoers to characters inclusive of Bugs

Bunny, Mickey Mouse, Daffy Duck, Donald Duck, and lots of others. Other live-movement shorts might also have featured the Three Stooges or the Little Rascals.

In the afternoons, many theaters confirmed a matinee. These have been cost effectively-made movies supposed for kids. Most were technological knowledge fiction or cowboy movies. Many of these films were serials, which means that each film must result in a "cliff-hanger", and more youthful website online visitors may also must return the subsequent week to appearance the belief. Matinees were commonly priced lower, with tickets costing as little as 10 cents. In the night, charge tag charges averaged approximately 25 cents, and theaters showed better first-rate films supposed for the entire own family.

Movies meant a exceptional deal to the human beings residing via the Great Depression. It was no longer in reality a form of enjoyment or a manner to skip the time.

Going to the movies supplied an awful lot needed comfort from the struggles of daily life. Many people had been horrible, and times have been hard, however for 25 cents, they will enter a lovely theater and neglect their troubles for multiple hours.

Bing Crosby

Bing Crosby have become a determine of famous subculture for nearly 3 a long term. Who changed into Bing Crosby? What did he do to come to be so well-known?

In 1903, in Tacoma, Washington, Harry and Kate Crosby gave start to a son, Harry Crosby Jr. When more younger Harry turn out to be six, he earned the nickname "Bingo". Over the direction of time, the "o" become dropped from this nickname, and he in reality have grow to be called Bing Crosby.

Bing have end up worried in song at the identical time as in immoderate university. He achieved drums for a quick-lived band made up of various excessive faculty college students. After immoderate college, he moved straight away to short achievement, making a song with Paul Whiteman's Orchestra for $one hundred and fifty each week. He then have end up the featured singer of the Rhythm Boys. It become with this company that Bing sang his first #1 hit, a jazz version of "Ol' Man River."

Crosby made his solo debut in September of 1931, and he quickly have come to be recognized for his one-of-a-type vocal competencies. His deep baritone voice entranced tens of tens of tens of millions of listeners. By the surrender of 1931, ten of the pinnacle 50 songs on the radio featured Bing Crosby.

In 1932, Bing starred in his first function film. The film turn out to be titled The Big Broadcast and became the number one of many movies starring Crosby. Bing would possibly pass straight away to turn out to be as well-known for his performing abilities as he changed into for his creating a track capabilities.

Crosby also had one of the most well-known radio indicates. Starting in 1936, he started out out internet hosting the Kraft Music Hall at the NBC Radio Network. He held this feature for the following ten years, fun listeners within the path of America, similarly to foreign places.

During the years of World War II, Bing's publicizes were transmitted to troops stopping in Europe and the Pacific. These announces were moreover heard via the usage of countless German troops who have grow to be enthusiasts as well, calling him "Der Bingle". Crosby moreover flew to Europe and made some of live appearances for infantrymen stationed there. Between his proclaims and stay performances, he boosted the morale of many soldiers and helped them enjoy a bit closer to domestic.

Bing Crosby's legacy as a performer is in reality unequalled. As a singer, he recorded greater than 1,seven-hundred songs. Forty-this type of reached #1 on the famous tune charts. His maximum famous recording is the song "White Christmas", which remains the superb-selling track of all time.

Crosby is also one of the most a hit actors of all-time. He seemed in a entire of 79 movies. More than 1 billion tickets had been presented to see films starring Bing Crosby. By this diploma, it ranks him because the 1/three most a achievement actor of all-time, inside the decrease again of Clark Gable and John Wayne. He received the Academy Award for Best Actor for his feature in Going My Way. He became also nominated for the award on different events. Many of his movies are appeared as classics these days, and they are capable of no matter the truth that be seen on tv.

Bing Crosby died on October 14, 1977, but he will hold to stay on within the hearts and minds of human beings round the arena for destiny years. A track emerge as as quickly as written in tribute to Bing which stated "Bing has a way of creating a song along together with his very coronary coronary heart and soul, which captivates the arena. His hundreds of thousands of listeners in no manner fail to have amusing at his golden voice."

Shirley Temple

During the 1930s, a more youthful actress named Shirley Temple extraordinarily blissful moviegoers in some unspecified time inside the destiny of the dominion. Why come to be Shirley Temple so famous? How is she remembered these days?

Shirley Temple have grow to be born in 1928 and commenced out out appearing almost as rapid as she have to stroll. Her first performing roles came in 1932 whilst she modified into handiest 3 years antique! By 1934, she have become a first-rate movie star. The movie Stand Up and Cheer! Added her to country wide interest. That same 12 months, the film Bright Eyes featured the tune "On the Good Ship Lollipop", that have come to be her signature music.

Throughout the relaxation of the closing decade, Shirley Temple have come to be one in all the most important stars in Hollywood. She starred in twenty special films from 1934 to 1939. The Little Colonel, Curly Top, The Littlest Rebel, Dimples, Heidi, and The Little Princess were just a few of the movies that propelled her to worldwide reputation.

Most of her movie roles had been very comparable. She modified into typically the little female with the intense smile who have to win over the hearts of the stingiest misers and soften the most calloused of people. She ought to reunite couples or remedy a few exclusive problem that came alongside. The movies typically featured many tune and dance numbers in which Shirley ought to display off her abilties. These heartwarming recollections provided a good deal desired idea for masses viewers who've been enduring the woes of the Great Depression.

Throughout the Thirties, many merchandise had been marketed offering Shirley's likeness. From Shirley Temple dolls to mugs and cereal bowls, she became everywhere. Other items that bore her name protected a line of Shirley Temple clothes, cleaning cleaning soap, sheet music, mirrors, and severa precise products.

Temple remained an active actress at a few degree in the Nineteen Forties and 50s, appearing in some of films and tv applications. However, she may also need to by no means be as a success as she have become sooner or later of the remaining decade of the 1930s. She retired from appearing and characteristic come to be an ambassador for the us. She changed into ambassador to Ghana from 1974 to 1976 and then to Czechoslovakia from 1989 to 1992.

Shirley Temple died in February of 2014 on the age of eighty 5. To in the period in-between, she stays one of the maximum loved performers within the history of the motion image organisation. Her films are nevertheless cherished with the beneficial aid of tens of millions of adoring enthusiasts, and he or she or he or he'll keep to stay on as a preferred piece of American statistics.

Will Rogers

One of the most enduring figures of the Thirties became Will Rogers. Who was Will Rogers? What did he end up well-known for?

Will Rogers became born in 1879 in Indian Territory, close to present-day Oologah, Oklahoma. His parents had been every detail Cherokee. He changed into the youngest of eight youngsters, but simplest 3 of his siblings survived into adulthood.

In 1901, Rogers heard that there has been coins to be made in Argentina. So, he and a friend headed out looking for their fortunes. When they arrived in Argentina, they determined that the cash they dreamed of emerge as a fable. His friend all over again to Oklahoma, but Will stayed. From there, he got a task on a ship that grow to be headed for South Africa.

In South Africa, he went to work on a ranch and became in the end hired through way of Texas Jack's Wild West Show. He appeared in the shows as "The Cherokee Kid" and feature become famous for acting rope pointers. He toured South Africa with the Wild West Show till he have become employed via a circus that took him to Australia and New Zealand.

In 1904, he lower lower back to the usa and started out acting vaudeville in New York City. Vaudeville have end up a shape of variety display which typically featured singers, dancers, jugglers, comedians, and precise performers. Rogers finished his recommendations and instructed jokes to the audience as he twirled his rope. The brand new New York audiences cherished Will's u . S . A . Accent. He additionally had a herbal sense of humor that crowds desired. Rogers might regularly open each show through using announcing, "All I recognize is what I observe in the papers". He might also then comedian tale approximately modern-day occasions and poke amusing at political figures of the era.

By 1916, he changed into the megastar of the maximum crucial display in New York, the Ziegfeld Follies. He additionally started acting in silent films, which only increased his superstar repute. In his movies, he occasionally portrayed cowboys, or likely comedic characters much like himself. He endured appearing in movies up thru 1935, ultimately starring in over fifty films.

Chapter 7: The Dust Bowl

The Dust Bowl became a excessive period of drought and dust storms in some unspecified time in the future of the 1930s. Why did the Dust Bowl display up? How excessive have become the damage?

The earliest explorers to the Great Plains place of North America determined that the region modified into improper for agriculture. The territory even became known as "The Great American Desert" because the dearth of wood and water made the location specially unattractive for agreement. However, inside the a long term following the Civil War, farmers started out to settle the location and domesticate the fields beneath the long-held, but wrong, belief that "rain will take a look at the plow."

In the first three a long term of the 1900s, there have been massive and non-forestall advances in farming generation, which includes better tractors, mechanized plowing, combines, and additional. From 1900 to 1920, the amount of farmland in the plains region doubled, and from 1925 to 1930, the amount of cultivated land tripled!

However, farmers of the technology used practices which deprived the soil of its vitamins and improved the opportunity of erosion. The heavy plowing had removed the herbal grasses of the prairie that held the soil in region and maintained moisture.

Then, in 1930, a immoderate drought struck the Great Plains region, which lasted nearly the whole decade. The regions affected most by the usage of this drought have been the panhandles of Texas and Oklahoma, western Kansas, and massive portions of Colorado and New Mexico. The more than a million acres that have come to be affected have grow to be together called "The Dust Bowl".

As the drought grew worse, the topsoil grew to come to be to dirt and blew away. The blowing dirt generated awesome dirt storms that reached as a long way east as

Washington D.C.! The dirt storms have come to be known as "black blizzards".

During the closing decade of the 1930s, the Dust Bowl location received anywhere from 15-25% tons less precipitation than regular. For an area that only sees approximately twenty inches of rain a yr, because of this some regions had been receiving as low as fifteen inches of rain in one year (in a few years, even an awful lot much less than that!).

As the last decade wore on, and the severity of the Dust Bowl superior, efforts were made to accurate the situations. The Civilian Conservation Corps planted more than hundred million timber from Texas to Canada in an attempt to block the wind and preserve the soil in location.

Farmers had been moreover suggested in soil conservation techniques collectively with crop rotation, contour plowing, and terracing. In some instances, the government even paid farmers a dollar an acre to workout this form of conservation strategies. By the prevent of the Thirties, that they had succeeded in lowering the amount of blowing dirt thru sixty five%.

By the time the rainfall decrease lower back to ordinary tiers, almost seventy five% of the topsoil were blown away in some regions. It might be years earlier than the region recovered completely.

Black Blizzards

During the 1930s, dust storms ravaged the Great Plains vicinity. The worst of these became called Black Sunday. When did Black Sunday take place? Just how lousy became it?

In the early a part of the twentieth Century, over-farming, awful soil conservation strategies, and immoderate farm animals grazing had created a volatile situation. The topsoil of the Great Plains place had been stripped of its vitamins, further to the herbal plants that had as quick as held the soil in area.

Then, 1930 observed the primary yr of what may also eventually be an 11 twelve months drought, wherein precipitation (inside the shape of rainfall, snow fall, and extremely good styles of moisture) changed into just a fraction of the ordinary stages.

These elements combined to dehydrate the soil and turn it proper into a pleasing, powdery dust. The wind picked up large portions of this dirt and generated massive dust storms which swept during the plains. The storms must achieve more than 10,000 feet in pinnacle and bring winds from 50 to eighty miles in step with hour. The storms came to be known as "black blizzards".

The dust storms began out in the early 1930s and persisted to development in severity and in variety due to the fact the final decade wore on. In 1932, there were at the least fourteen fundamental dirt storms, through way of way of 1935 there have been extra than forty, and 1937 observed greater than seventy. Historical statistics of the generation had been now not stored because it should be, and a few speculate that there may also had been multiple hundred dust storms in three hundred and sixty 5 days.

The worst of these dirt storms took place on April 14, 1935. The typhoon blew away an anticipated 3 hundred million masses of topsoil in only a few days. The sky have turn out to be so complete of dust, that the solar couldn't be seen. Some witnesses defined the event as "a wall of dirt that the eyes could not penetrate". This typhoon have turn out to be called "Black Sunday".

Chapter 8: Dust Pneumonia & Dust Storm Preparations

One of the worst fitness conditions from the Dust Bowl technology have end up dirt pneumonia. What turned into dust pneumonia? What techniques did Dust Bowl residents use to try and combat the encroaching dirt?

During the Thirties, at the same time as the Great Plains place changed into being plagued via a drought and ravaged through dirt storms, a brand new bodily ailment emerged. It have become called dust pneumonia, and it have become because of inhaling dirt from the air. Dirt would possibly fill the lungs and reason coughing, tightness of the chest, labored respiratory, and shortness of breath.

Children and the aged were affected the most, with deaths being commonplace. Many had been hospitalized because of this example, but it's far tough to inform proper numbers due to the fact medical facts from the generation have been each not stored, or not well preserved.

Those who lived inside the Dust Bowl attempted many techniques to combat the dust and hold themselves healthful.

Parents might also want to have their children sleep with sheets over their beds, like a tent, to lessen the quantity of dust they inhaled in the course of their sleep. Dust mask and wet cloths over the mouth had been different strategies that a few used to try to prevent dust inhalation. Additionally, goggles have been now and again worn to hold blowing dust out of the eyes.

Housewives made many efforts to maintain the dirt and dirt out of the residence. Sometimes those sports were as smooth as continuously sweeping the floors. Other methods have been extra large, which includes tacking bed sheets in front of doorways and domestic domestic home windows, wetting them down an excellent manner to maintain out as a whole lot dirt as possible. They drastically applied strips of cloth, soaked in a paste crafted from flour and water, to insulate the outer edges of domestic home windows, trying to seal them near.

While human beings need to take the ones measures, animals have been not so lucky. Cattle and one-of-a-type livestock had little shelter and nowhere to run from the dirt storms. Many households were compelled to examine helplessly as their animals died from dirt inhalation. No livestock meant no meat, eggs, milk, or one in every of a type dairy merchandise, which extraordinary delivered more difficulty to their lives.

The dust changed into anywhere. Residents of the Dust Bowl vicinity lived in it, breathed it, slept in it, and even ate it (many Dust Bowl survivors testify that they might enjoy the gritty dirt in their food). There become no escaping it. The measures mentioned above helped reduce the dirt a few, but it modified into a ordinary presence of their lives.

Rabbits, Grasshoppers

& Other Problems

The dust and dirt storms of the Dust Bowl technology were sincerely the start of farmers' issues in the Thirties. What had been a number of the opposite troubles they faced?

As a immoderate drought ravaged the Great Plains, and the big dust storms further altered the ecology of the location, new waves of pests started out out sweeping at some stage in the prairie.

The worst of those new varmints have been jackrabbits. Jackrabbits breed at an super fee, producing as many as 8 more youthful a month. Normally, jackrabbit populations are kept at regular tiers because of their natural predators together with coyotes. However, in the course of the Dust Bowl, those predators had each died, or moved right away to distinct areas seeking out water.

With no herbal predators, the jackrabbit populace surged to fantastic levels, and that they have grow to be a notable pest during the plains as they ate grass and vegetation. In an attempt to reduce the jackrabbit population, residents for the duration of the Dust Bowl region held rabbit drives, rounding up the animals and removing them. In one rabbit force, which occurred in Kansas, they captured more than 35,000 rabbits in a single afternoon.

Grasshoppers have grow to be some different nightmare at some stage in the Dust Bowl. Just just like the jackrabbits, the grasshopper's natural predators (birds and rodents) had moved on on the lookout for water. Grasshoppers travelled in swarms at a few degree in the land, with as many as 23,000 bugs consistent with acre. They gobbled in truth the whole thing in their course.

Many efforts were implemented to attempt to curtail the plague of grasshoppers. The National Guard burned infested fields and even crushed the insects with tractors. The

Civilian Conservation Corps spread big portions of insecticide which emerge as crafted from arsenic, molasses, and bran.

Inside homes, distinct varieties of bugs have been a risk as well. Poisonous centipedes and deadly spiders infiltrated homes attempting to find shade or water. There are some reviews of ladies filling whole buckets complete of these forms of pests.

Static energy created a selected form of chance. Friction due to blowing dirt particles rubbing together, and in opposition to metallic devices, created large quantities of static power. This strength modified into powerful sufficient to kill flora or even knock a person unconscious. Many Dust Bowl survivors maintain in mind seeing blue arcs of static energy at night time time, coming from windmills and barbed twine fences. These were just a few of the more dangers that many people persevered at some level within the Dust Bowl.

Okies

As the Dust Bowl made existence an increasing number of hard for the ones dwelling within the precious plains, many humans decided to desert their homes in search of new opportunities. Who had been those humans? Where did they skip?

Many left the Dust Bowl location in opt for of seeking out a hobby within the metropolis. Others decided to head away the area altogether. Most of folks who left had a common tour spot, California. Writers of the era found that the highways amongst Oklahoma and California resembled a parade, with a non-stop string of motors heading west. Others compared it to the gold rush of 1849, with hundreds and heaps of migrants shifting searching out a smooth begin.

In 1934 by myself, Oklahoma misplaced more than four hundred,000 people. That identical 12 months, Kansas out of location over 200,000. The plains states as an entire professional a lack of 2.Five million humans. Oklahoma suffered the most in terms of population loss. Other states out of place 3% or four% in their population, however a few estimates claim that Oklahoma misplaced as plenty as 18% of its general population.

Not all of the Dust Bowl refugees were from Oklahoma, but because so pretty some them were, the Californians had a nickname for all of them. They known as them Okies. Journalist Ben Reddick first used the term "Okie" in his articles after noticing the "OK" abbreviation at the diverse migrant license plates.

Most of these Okies had been heading to California due to the fact they idea they'll discover jobs deciding on fruit. After all, California furnished almost 1/2 of of the clean fruit for the entire united states. However, there had been multiple downsides to this career.

First, there have been far greater employees than have been desired. With the sort of surplus of employees, employers need to pay extremely low wages (there has been no minimum income at that point). Additionally, many roles handiest lasted or three days, at which element the employee needed to circulate without delay to the following location on the way to discover more art work. This pressured the Okies right into a migratory lifestyle, continuously moving straight away to the following orchard, grove, or winery.

Given the migrant manner of lifestyles and coffee pay, the Okies lived a completely tough, ugly lifestyles. They were regarded down upon via Californians and many towns refused to permit them the front. They have been forced to stay out of doors of groups in makeshift villages of shacks and other poorly built shelters. These locations have become called Little Oklahomas. Because those groups have been filthy, with little proper sanitation and no on foot water, diseases collectively with typhus and diphtheria have turn out to be enormous.

To help expose the plight of the Okies, a writer named John Steinbeck wrote a e-book in 1939 titled The Grapes of Wrath. This novel informed the tale of Tom Joad and his circle of relatives as they traveled from Oklahoma to California and their hardships after they arrived.

Eventually, the U.S. Government attempted to assist the Okies living in California. Camps had been organized to offer higher rest room and bathing centers similarly to community cooking regions and laundry rooms. By 1941, there were thirteen of these camps inside the route of California with approximately 45,000 humans residing in them.

The nickname "Okie" changed into at the start used by Californians as an insult. In The Grapes of Wrath, the primary man or woman Tom Joad located, "Okie way you're scum." However, in modern-day instances, many human beings from Oklahoma have embraced the nickname and use it with pride, clearly as a Hoosier from Indiana or a Yankee from New England makes use of those nicknames.

The Grapes of Wrath

In 1939, John Steinbeck wrote a unique which would possibly become one of the maximum arguable books of all time. It could additionally become one of the maximum celebrated works of American literature. What modified into this novel? Why changed into it so debatable?

The Grapes of Wrath specializes within the Joad own family, horrible sharecroppers from Oklahoma who've to leave their domestic because of the Dust Bowl and the opposite monetary hardships related to the Great Depression. In an try and exchange their unique fortune, they set out for California, in conjunction with lots of other Okies.

The e-book modified into first posted on March 14, 1939. By May, it have become at the top of the excellent dealers list, and through way of the give up of 1939, nearly

500,000 copies have been bought. Its rate of $2.Seventy five became pretty reasonable on the time, which allowed many humans to buy copies. Even folks who had in no way have a look at a ebook before were looking for it. Book stores have been offered out, and there had been organized lists at libraries which have been months prolonged.

The ebook paints a absolutely shiny photo of the hardships persisted with the aid of manner of the Dust Bowl's migrant human beings. It moreover illustrates how the migrants were treated after arriving in California. When human beings test it, they were greatly surprised with the resource of way of the poverty and hopelessness furnished inside the story.

However, now not every person favored what they had been reading. There had been claims that the e-book exaggerated the hardships of the Okies. Many declared that it come to be impossible for such horrible conditions to exist in the United States of America. Also, citizens of California had been displeased with the manner Steinbeck portrayed the Californian attitude within the direction of the migrants. The Associated Farmers of California denounced the ebook as a % of lies.

Some criticized the novel for wonderful reasons. It emphasized cooperative solutions to economic problems as opposed to individualistic solutions. Because of those issue subjects, many humans felt it changed into seasoned-socialist or seasoned-communist.

Because of the book's debatable nature, it emerge as banned from many libraries at some point of the us of a. One institution in California called for "large denouncement in opposition to the e-book earlier than university opens and our boys and women find out such filthy material on the shelves of our public library."

National radio packages debated the deserves of the ebook, and it changed into even publicly burned in Buffalo, New York; East St.

Louis, Illinois; and in numerous corporations in California. Oklahoma Representative Lyle Boren went as a protracted way as denouncing the e-book in Congress as a vulgar lie. However, an lousy lot of this uproar died down while Eleanor Roosevelt praised the ebook and defended Steinbeck.

In 1939, The Grapes of Wrath gained the Pulitzer Prize for a Novel, and the popularity of the ebook has persevered to in recent times. John Steinbeck's novel has been translated into many superb languages including French, German, and Japanese.

The Grapes of Wrath stays banned in lots of college libraries during the dominion. However, it is probably the maximum noted and debated American novel of the twentieth Century and could usually be considered one of the classics of American literature.

John Steinbeck

John Steinbeck became considered one of America's best authors. What books did John

Steinbeck write? Why had been they so famous?

Raised in California, John Steinbeck normal an appreciation for the place. In unique, he grew to like California's Salinas Valley, which substantially recommended his writing. As a youngster, Steinbeck made the selection to turn out to be a author and regularly locked himself in his room to do his writing. In 1919, Steinbeck enrolled at Stanford University, but in the end dropped out in 1925, having in no manner graduated.

Steinbeck in quick moved to New York City in which he determined art work as a newspaper reporter, but the pull of California short drew him back home. While taking walks as a caretaker in Lake Tahoe, he wrote his first novel, Cup of Gold, in 1929. Over the following decade Steinbeck wrote The Pastures of Heaven and To a God Unknown, each of which were poorly acquired via way of critics.

Steinbeck eventually completed achievement with Tortilla Flat in 1935, a humorous novel about existence inside the Monterrey area. The e-book became very popular, selling more than 26,000 copies in its first three hundred and sixty five days (sooner or later of the heart of the Depression). Two years later, Steinbeck published Of Mice and Men. This novel tells the tale of migrant ranch personnel. Much of the e-book is based mostly on Steinbeck's own studies touring america of the usa as a hobo. Of Mice and Men stays notably famous and is study in lecture rooms throughout the kingdom.

The Grapes of Wrath have become posted in 1939. The novel relays the story of a Depression-era Oklahoma circle of relatives and their conflict to create a modern life in California. In many minds, it perfectly captured the mood and discontent of the kingdom in some unspecified time in the future of this difficult time. At one factor, The Grapes of Wrath have turn out to be promoting 10,000 copies consistent with week! It moreover earned Steinbeck a Pulitzer Prize in 1940.

Following the success of The Grapes of Wrath, Steinbeck served as a warfare correspondent within the course of World War II. He continued to put in writing for the rest of his lifestyles, producing classics which includes Cannery Row and East of Eden. He became even provided the Nobel Prize for Literature in 1962.

John Steinbeck died of coronary heart sickness on December 20, 1968, however left in the again of a massive legacy that included 27 books. Over a 10 3 hundred and sixty five days length, he produced severa of America's greatest masterpieces of fiction. He will constantly be remembered for writing approximately social and monetary issues whilst giving voice to walking-beauty America. He is one from an elite listing of authors who had a present for developing characters that have been relatable to a extensive, fashionable target market.

Woody Guthrie

Unquestionably, the maximum enduring musical discern to emerge from the Dust Bowl era have emerge as a man named Woody Guthrie. Why become Woody so famous? What form of songs did he sing?

Woody Guthrie turned into born in Okemah, Oklahoma in 1912. His father turn out to be the number one County Clerk in Okfuskee County. By the necessities of the day, his family was a median, middleclass circle of relatives.

Chapter 9: The Kingfish

Throughout the Great Depression, there were many humans searching out solutions. They have been organized to take a look at in reality anyone who might also additionally have an clean therapy for the dominion's woes. One of these guys end up Huey P. Long. Who have become this guy? What had been his answers?

During the 1930s, many politicians, tough paintings leaders, and preachers were growing a name for themselves. They used all of us's fear, tension, and anger as a device to climb thru the ranks of power. Many of these leaders have become called "demagogues". The most distinguished of the demagogues became Huey P. Long, nicknamed "the Kingfish".

Huey Long modified into born in 1893. He grew up in a completely horrible area of Louisiana, yet his circle of relatives have become pretty properly off. He studied law at Tulane University and jumped proper into politics at an early age. He ran for governor in 1924 and out of place, then ran again in 1928 and acquired. In 1930, he ran for the U.S. Senate and won that too! By 1935, he have become without troubles the high-quality guy inside the u . S . Of Louisiana.

Economic conditions were terrible in Louisiana within the 1930s. Long achieved heaps of his fulfillment with the aid of way of way of attractive to terrible farmers and production unit people with a "awful in opposition to the rich" mentality. He additionally delivered on some of the guarantees he had made at some point of his advertising marketing campaign. These ensures blanketed paving roads and constructing public schools. He knowledgeable his fanatics that 65% of the united states of america's wealth have become controlled thru 2% of the populace. He preached a message that "each guy is a king, however nobody wears a crown," and often used the slogan "Share the Wealth".

Long argued that there have to be limits located on how lots wealth someone ought to collect. Anything past that diploma can be redistributed to others. He believed that each deserving circle of relatives have to acquire $5,000. He promised that below his device, every own family is probably confident an annual profits of $2,000 to $3,000, a 30 hour paintings week, one month of vacation a 12 months, vintage age pensions, and unfastened college schooling for deserving college university college students.

Suddenly, "Share the Wealth" golf equipment started out out bobbing up all over the u . S . A .. There have been more than 27,000 golf equipment with over four.6 million contributors. He obtained plenty of letters of help from at some stage in the kingdom. As the Kingfish's message persisted to unfold, he commenced to set his factors of interest on the huge prize— being elected President of the united states. Long modified into not nice famous in his home united states, but had huge quantities of help at some point of the us of america.

However, on September eight, 1935, Long had back to Louisiana. As he changed into strolling towards the governor's workplace, a person in a white match stepped out from within the lower back of a pillar and fired a unmarried shot into Senator Long. Long's bodyguards opened fireplace and gunned down the assassin, leaving sixty one bullets inside the gunman's frame. Long come to be rushed to a sanatorium in which he died 30 hours later.

Tens of masses of Louisianans grew to turn out to be out for the Kingfish's funeral. His lack of existence changed into mourned with the aid of people inside the direction of the kingdom. He changed into buried on the grounds of the u . S . Capitol constructing, which now has a statue offering his likeness. He has furthermore been commemorated with a statue within the United States Capitol Building.

John L. Lewis

One of the maximum influential exertions leaders of the Nineteen Thirties have become John L. Lewis. Who emerge as John L. Lewis? How did he emerge as so influential?

John L. Lewis grow to be born in Iowa in 1880. His father have become a coal miner, and Lewis himself went to paintings in the coal mines at the same time as he become first-class sixteen. He have grow to be lively in the coal miner's union and in the end worked carefully with Samuel Gompers (the founder of the American Federation of Labor).

In the 1930s, there were few industries as essential because the coal organisation. However, coalminers were not allowed to enroll inside the AFL because it become created for "professional employee's" and coalminers had been "unskilled worker's". As a end cease end result, Lewis normal the Congress of Industrial Organizations (CIO). This have become a conglomerate difficult paintings union product of other exertions unions which all represented unskilled people. This protected not only coalminers, however rubber employees (who made tires), metallic personnel, car personnel, and plenty of others.

The CIO supported many organizations of placing personnel inside the late Nineteen Thirties. One of the most important movements of the closing decade turned into a strike via manner of the United Auto Workers. The General Motors factories in Flint, Michigan and Cleveland, Ohio were clearly near down through the placing employees. Before the strike, the GM factories have been producing 15,000 motors every week. During the strike, this range dropped to truely over 100 fifty. GM have turn out to be in the end pressured to barter with its hanging personnel for better wages and extra steady operating conditions.

This became in reality really one in every of many actions which happened within the latter half of of of the Nineteen Thirties, all of that have been sponsored thru using John L. Lewis and the CIO. Other moves passed off in steel mills, tire factories, shoe factories, plane factories, and even bakeries. Many of these strikes were not traditional moves, in which employees walked out, or protested on wood strains. Instead, they used a modern method of setting known as the sit down down down-in, or take a seat-down strike.

The humans may want to occupy their ordinary workspace, however surely refuse to art work. This had the benefit of creating it difficult for police or National Guard to dispose of them, and it made it in reality no longer possible for the humans to get replaced. It additionally extended camaraderie some of the people as they have been dwelling together inside the production unit for days, or perhaps weeks (for example, the GM factory strike lasted forty four days!). In an try to skip the time in the route of the take a seat down-in, personnel would possibly play gambling playing cards or take note of the radio. One strike even featured a band which finished for the hanging employees (the band itself modified into fabricated from human beings). Meals might be delivered in through better halves or friends who've been helping their cause.

Through the ones efforts, the human beings professional a modern day enjoy of power. They were able to effect trade of their situation and offer a better strolling surroundings and higher wages for their fellow workers.

Many of these movements had been made feasible, or closely supported, with the aid of using the efforts of John L. Lewis and the Congress of Industrial Organizations. Lewis would in all likelihood stay a chief determine in American hard artwork for the following a long time. He is remembered in recent times as one of the maximum critical figures of the twentieth Century tough paintings movement.

1930s Religion

& Father Coughlin

The era of the Great Depression observed an boom in the workout of religion. Why did this increase get up? Who modified into the crucial chief of the movement?

As monetary hardships persevered to get worse at a few degree within the 1930s, many people started out to keep tightly to their religion. For them, conditions had turn out to be so miserable that their only want modified into that some component masses better awaited them after lack of life. Religion have end up an emotional stabilizer and helped many humans via the difficult instances.

Between 1929 and 1937 there has been a sharp upward thrust in all the Protestant denominations of Christianity. Methodists, Baptists, Lutherans, and loads of diverse churches all skilled a shocking boom in membership. Catholic church attendance have become on the upward push as well. Several new spiritual corporations, which incorporates the Jehovah's Witnesses, moreover emerged for the duration of the Thirties.

Millions of humans determined comfort and safety within the church network. Historically, providing aid to the awful had normally been a mission fulfilled by way of the usage of church homes. Soup kitchens, food and clothing donations, and different alleviation efforts had been all organized thru severa non secular companies at a few diploma within the kingdom.

One of the leaders of this new non secular fervor became Father Charles Coughlin. Father Coughlin served because the priest for a Catholic church in Michigan known as the Shrine of the Little Flower. He also hosted a radio software program known as The Radio League of the Little Flower. As the Thirties advanced, Father Coughlin have turn out to be one of the maximum listened to voices on the radio.

Chapter 10: Alfalfa Bill Murray

One of the maximum charismatic and arguable governors of the Nineteen Thirties turn out to be Governor William H. Murray from Oklahoma. What did Murray do to emerge as so well-known? Why did he end up arguable?

William H. Murray have become born in Toadsuck, Texas on November 21, 1869. The own family moved to Montague, Texas after his mother died and his father remarried. At the age of twelve, more youthful Bill determined to go away domestic. He modified into in the long run located with the resource of some other circle of relatives who had him attending college inside the iciness and running on farms all through the summer time.

As he got older, he labored as a salesclerk, a instructor, a newspaper reporter, and a criminal professional. But, he changed into first and maximum vital a farmer. He continuously liked to inform human beings that he "believed inside the circle of relatives farm, the values of Thomas Jefferson, and the greatness of the Democratic Party."

In 1898, Murray moved to Tishomingo, which changed into the capital of the Chickasaw Nation in Indian Territory. He have become concerned in politics on the same time as dwelling in Indian Territory and served as one of the representatives at the Sequoyah Convention. This have become a meeting which tried to create a country out of Indian Territory (the japanese half of of present-day Oklahoma).

Murray have grow to be additionally president of the constitutional conference when Oklahoma in the end have grow to be a nation in 1907. He changed into the usa of a's first Speaker of the House, a member of Congress, and he ran for governor instances and misplaced, all in advance than 1924. Bill Murray regarded to be a regular parent in Oklahoma politics. In a lot of his speeches, he often stated a plot of land which he grew alfalfa on. One newspaper stated him as "Alfalfa Bill" in a column. The nickname stayed with him at some stage in the remainder of his existence.

Then, in 1924, Murray and his partner led a tough and fast of American colonists, most of them Oklahomans, to Bolivia. Once they had been in Bolivia, they attempted to installation an agrarian colony. The try failed miserably, and handiest five years later, in 1929, they again to Oklahoma.

Alfalfa Bill had out of place all of his cash within the attempt. So, he borrowed $forty from a monetary group in Tishomingo and began a advertising and marketing marketing marketing campaign for governor. Murray traveled in the course of the u . S . In a tired vehicle, preventing at road corners to offer speeches. He ate his lunch out of a paper bag at the equal time as talking about politics with absolutely everyone who could likely concentrate. He became frequently unshaven and his clothes had been grimy. He supplied himself as a right proper right down to earth not unusual guy. He gained the 1930 election by way of manner of extra than 100,000 votes, becoming Oklahoma's ninth governor. This have turn out to be the most critical victory of any Oklahoma governor as a bargain as that factor.

During his profession as governor, Murray known as out the National Guard on forty seven sports and declared martial regulation 30 instances. The most well-known of these grow to be the two month incident known as the "Toll Bridge War". In the summer season of 1931, Oklahoma National Guardsmen faced off in opposition to Texas Rangers over a "free bridge" which have been constructed across the Red River to update an older toll bridge. When the governor of Texas, Ross Sterling, sent Rangers to barricade the Texas side of the brand new bridge (as a part of a courtroom docket injunction), Governor Murray despatched National Guardsmen to do away with the barricades and maintain roads to the bridge open. The Texas injunction in opposition to the ultra-modern-day bridge was ultimately dissolved.

As governor, Murray have turn out to be one of the early countrywide leaders in the try to help the ones damage through the Great Depression. He used his personal income to feed the terrible and collected coins from united states employees and businessmen to finance comfort applications to beneficial aid those struggling throughout the economic crisis.

Alfalfa Bill's recognition even carried him onto the national scene. In 1932, he tried to turn out to be the Democrat nominee for president. He participated in severa primary elections, but in the long run lost the nomination to Franklin D. Roosevelt.

Eleanor Roosevelt

Eleanor Roosevelt grow to be one of the most influential First Ladies in American information. What did she do that modified the position of the First Lady? How did she effect American life?

Eleanor Roosevelt become raised in New York City. Her family changed into specifically rich, however her adolescence come to be no longer with out its issues. Both her parents died earlier than she turn out to be 10. When Eleanor end up 18, she met her future husband, Franklin, at the same time as journeying on a train. Eventually, the two had been engaged, and they married on March 17, 1905.

Eleanor's feature in politics started out out as early as 1921 on the onset of Franklin's polio. She would possibly fill in for him at public appearances even as he became incapable of travelling. She additionally have emerge as a sturdy propose for such dreams as minimal revenue, a 48 hour art work week, and the abolition of toddler hard work.

Chapter 11: Margaret Mitchell & Gone With The Wind

One of the most drastically-examine novels of the Nineteen Thirties modified into Gone with the Wind. Who wrote this novel? Why changed into it so well-known?

Margaret Mitchell lived her whole existence in Atlanta, Georgia. She grow to be born right into a wealthy circle of relatives in 1900. Her father have become a legal expert, and her mother come to be a suffragist who fought for girls's rights.

Margaret changed into a tomboy who preferred using ponies over playing with dolls. When she modified into little, she must cross using nearly every day with a Confederate veteran. At the age of six, Margaret's mom took her on a tour of many of the plantations that have been burned, or in any other case destroyed, inside the direction of the Civil War. As a infant, she furthermore spent lots time round uncles who had been Civil War veterans and aunts who had lived through the warfare. These elderly circle of relatives knowledgeable her many testimonies about the warfare and the manner tough the ones times had been. When Margaret changed into 22, she took a activity as a journalist on the Atlanta Journal. Her circle of relatives did no longer approve of this profession, as they felt being a author modified into underneath her fame in society. She labored for the Atlanta Journal for four years, writing extra than hundred articles.

Then, in 1926, she modified into worried in an vehicle accident that substantially injured her ankle. While enhancing, her husband advocated her to write down down a completely unique. She persisted to artwork on the manuscript for the subsequent ten years. Finally, in 1936, the novel have become published. It was titled Gone with the Wind.

Gone with the Wind tells the tale of Scarlett O'Hara, the daughter of a rich plantation owner, who famous herself in poverty in the aftermath of the Civil War. It's a coming-of-age story that information the struggles of Scarlett's existence as she grows from adolescence into adulthood.

The novel end up straight away successful, becoming the nice-selling book of each 1936 and 1937. People in the course of America, specially girls, were reading Gone with the Wind. It resonated with many that had professional prosperity at some degree inside the Twenties but determined themselves suffering within the midst of the Great Depression. In 1937, Mitchell obtained the Pulitzer Prize for fiction. Two years later, the film model have come to be released starring Clark Gable and Vivien Leigh. The film come to be a smashing fulfillment, putting field place of job facts that would stand for many years.

The novel might also sooner or later be translated into more than seventy languages. Foreign audiences appreciated the tale for its topics of love, battle, beauty war, racial strife, and generational conflict, that are sizable to the human circumstance.

To on the winning time, the radical remains loved and loved through the usage of lots and masses of readers within the path of the sector. It is concept of as one of the best American novels ever written, and a e-book that helped have an impact on and form the united states.

Amelia Earhart

One of the maximum famous female pilots who ever lived changed into Amelia Earhart. What did Amelia do to emerge as so well-known?

When Amelia Earhart have become approximately two a long time antique, she attended the Canadian National Exposition in Toronto. While there, she watched an aerial demonstration through a World War I pilot and became interested in airplanes. Two years later, in 1920, her father paid $10 for her to take a 10 minute flight that changed her existence. During this flight, she decided that she ought to discover ways to fly airplanes for herself. At the rate of $1,000, she signed up for flying instructions.

She fast proved to be a expert pilot or even set a global report. In 1922, she have become the primary female to fly at an altitude of 14,000 feet. The next one year, she received her pilot's license, becoming only the sixteenth woman to obtain this.

Over the subsequent numerous years, she did a considerable amount of flying. In 1928, she have become the primary woman to move the Atlantic Ocean in an plane. However, she have become now not the pilot in this adventure. She served because of the truth the navigator for pilot Wilmer Stultz. That identical year, she additionally became the number one girl to fly solo sooner or later of North America. These ambitious feats without issues made her the most well-known lady pilot of her day. One newspaper mentioned her as "Lady Lindy" (evaluating her to Charles Lindbergh), at the same time as some different called her "The Queen of the Air".

She fast became one of the chief spokespersons for the aviation agency.

On May 20, 1932, a 34-three hundred and sixty five days-antique Amelia Earhart took off from Harbour Grace, Newfoundland. She traveled for almost 15 hours, going via fierce north winds, mechanical problems, and volatile, icy flying situations. She touched down just north of Derry, in Northern Ireland. Her touchdown come to be best witnessed thru farmers. She had in truth turn out to be the primary girl to fly for the duration of the Atlantic Ocean on a solo flight.

In 1937, Earhart determined she should try to fly around the arena, a few component no girl had ever performed. She made her first attempt on March 17, 1937. Her plane took off in Oakland, California however high-quality made it as some distance as Honolulu, Hawaii earlier than experiencing mechanical troubles. The flight became called off and rescheduled.

The 2d strive came on June 1, 1937, this time departing from Miami, Florida. She and her navigator, Fred Noonan, had traveled greater than 22,000 miles even as some thing went horribly incorrect. Somewhere inside the center of the Pacific Ocean, they found out they were hopelessly out of place. On the morning of July 2, 1937, Amelia Earhart despatched out her closing radio message at 8:40 3 AM, indicating that they were on foot low on gas. A big are looking for lasted for seventeen days, however no wreckage became ever decided. Earhart and Noonan had been in no manner heard from over again.

Amelia Earhart turned into unsuccessful in flying spherical the arena, however her call remains remembered these days. She changed into the primary female to fly solo at some stage in the Atlantic Ocean, and she or he inspired a technology of ladies to obtain top notch heights in lots of one-of-a-kind fields.

Babe Didrikson Zaharias

One of the most remarkable athletes of the Nineteen Thirties changed into Babe Didrikson Zaharias. Who have become Babe? What sports activities did she come to be famous for?

Babe Didrikson's real name changed into Mildred, however nearly anyone recollects her as "Babe" (a lifelong nickname). Her parents had been Norwegian immigrants, and he or she or he had six brothers and sisters. When she have become four years vintage, her family moved to Beaumont, Texas in which she would possibly expand up. She wasn't a awesome student or maybe dropped out before finishing excessive college.

Fortunately for Babe, she modified into a very proficient athlete. When she was 21, she obtained global hobby at the Amateur Athletic Union (AAU) Championships in July of 1932. In much less than 3 hours, she competed in eight amazing sports, winning 5 and tying for first in a 6th. She set 3 worldwide records that day, collectively with the javelin, 80m hurdles, baseball throw (which she threw 272 ft), and the excessive bounce. Later that month, she competed in the 1932 Summer Olympics in Los Angeles. She obtained gold medals (the hurdles and javelin throw) and a silver for the excessive jump.

After the Olympics, she started a career in golfing. Throughout the late Nineteen Thirties and 1940s, Babe Didrikson changed into the dominant name in girls's golfing. She became virtually America's first woman golfing movie star. She accomplished many feats all through her profession, which encompass being the primary American to win the British Ladies Amateur. At one component she obtained as many as 13 tournaments in a row!

In 1938, she married a expert wrestler named George Zaharias, turning into Babe Didrikson Zaharias. The met at the same time as at a charity golf occasion and wed tons much less than a one year later. The couple remained married for the relaxation of Babe's lifestyles.

Aside from being a skilled music athlete and golfer, Babe Zaharias skilled first-rate fulfillment in specific sports sports sports as well. She finished baseball and softball, changed right into a expert diver, a bowler, and she or he or he or he also excelled at curler-skating. She additionally located time to be an superb seamstress, stitching all of her non-public golfing clothes. She may additionally want to even play the harmonica and sing (she recorded songs for Mercury Records!).

Chapter 12: Dorothea Lange

Some of the maximum lovable images from the Thirties have been excited about the useful aid of Dorothea Lange. Who changed into Dorothea Lange? Why have become she taking all the ones images?

Dorothea Lange turn out to be born in New Jersey in 1895. When she end up seven years vintage, she shriveled polio, which definitely weakened her proper leg. As a end cease end result, she walked with a limp for the remainder of her lifestyles.

She attended Columbia University wherein she took commands in photographs. She subsequently opened a portrait studio in San Francisco, but whilst the Great Depression struck, Lange began out photographing the homeless and unemployed she observed arriving in California.

Her pix of Dust Bowl refugees attracted the eye of government companies, and she or he changed into eventually hired with the resource of the Farm Security Administration (also referred to as the Resettlement Administration). She, alongside issue her husband, Paul Schuster Taylor, endured to file the destitute humans they encountered over the latter 1/2 of of the Thirties. Taylor come to be an economics professor who collected facts on the identical time as Lange photographed the human beings.

Many of Lange's images helped convey the plight of the terrible to country wide interest. The pictures regarded in newspapers and magazines throughout the u . S . A .. Her most well-known picture is entitled "Migrant Mother", which suggests a distraught woman and her youngsters.

In 1942, absolutely after the Japanese attack on Pearl Harbor, masses of Japanese Americans had been being pressured to relocate into internment camps. Once over again, Lange turned into there along facet her digital camera. She preserved images of Japanese Americans who had dedicated no crime but had been being detained with the useful resource of their personal u . S .. The US Army disapproved of her photographs and impounded them for thirty years.

Lange went directly to clearly take transport of a characteristic education pics on the California School of Fine Arts. Through the the rest of her existence, she struggled with some of health issues, which incorporates bleeding ulcers. She additionally suffered from renewed signs associated with her bout with polio. She died in 1965 at the age of 70, following a struggle with esophageal maximum cancers.

Dorothea Lange has been remembered in severa methods. A college near the spot wherein she photographed the "Migrant Mother" has been named in her honor. She has furthermore been inducted into the California Hall of Fame. Of route, her most lasting legacy will usually be the photographs she captured at some degree within the Nineteen Thirties and '40s, at the manner to hold to characteristic haunting reminders of those troubling times.

Federal Theatre Project

One of the maximum debatable New Deal programs became the Federal Theatre Project. What have become the Federal Theatre Project? Why become it debatable?

The Federal Theatre Project (FTP) modified into organized in August of 1935. Its intention changed into to lease as many out-of-work actors, directors, and artists as viable. Aside from employing the actors and different performers, the Federal Theatre Project moreover had the secondary mission of amusing the united states. Actors, singers, and dancers finished shows all throughout America, imparting a much wanted get away from the financial realities of the Great Depression.

In its four years, it employed 12,seven hundred personnel in 31 superb states. This application not simplest hired actors, however producers, directors, and script writers as properly. Carpenters have been employed to gather devices, seamstresses have been hired to design costumes, and unskilled people have been introduced in to be rate tag-takers or paintings backstage in masses of numerous capacities.

Several actors, writers, and directors who worked with the FTP might pass straight away to greater popularity later in their careers. Arthur Miller, John Houseman, and Orson Welles are just a few of the names who participated in FTP duties. Houseman and Welles, at the aspect of Marc Blitzstein, collaborated at the debatable FTP manufacturing titled The Cradle Will Rock.

The FTP produced extra than 1,two hundred plays and located on one thousand performances consistent with week. An expected 30 million humans saw FTP-produced performs. This gave the business company an extremely good amount of have an effect on over American opinion. This is why the employer have emerge as debatable as time superior.

Some felt that the performs and musicals produced thru the FTP had been a ways too politically opinionated. There were those in Congress who did not sense that a government enterprise need to be generating what they believed have turn out to be propaganda. For example, one production became extraordinarily important of the Supreme Court. Another production promoted employee rights and advocated humans to head on strike. One play, Revolt of the Beavers, became criticized for being seasoned-communist. Revolt of the Beavers turned into in particular troubling to many because it modified into centered mainly at children.

It was the controversial nature of those productions which in the end added approximately the surrender of the FTP. Congress disapproved of the program and cancelled its funding on June 30, 1939.

The World of Tomorrow

In 1939, the New York World's Fair gave spectators a glimpse at the "global of tomorrow". What became the World's Fair? What kinds of suggests have been there?

Throughout the Thirties, there were many expositions and "worldwide's festivals" throughout the dominion. One of the primary passed off in Philadelphia in 1926. It emerge as referred to as the Sesquicentennial International Exposition and celebrated the one hundred and fiftieth anniversary of the usa of the usa's independence. Chicago held a comparable event in 1933 referred to as the Century of Progress Exposition. California hosted two worldwide's gala's. The first became in 1935, in San Diego, and it have emerge as called the California Pacific Exposition. The 2d came in 1937 and modified into known as the Golden Gate Exposition, with the featured enchantment being the newly constructed Golden Gate Bridge.

The biggest and incredible of the area's gala's modified into the New York World's Fair which opened on April 30, 1939. The honest protected almost rectangular miles and had numerous zones, in conjunction with Transportation, Communications, Food, Government, Community Interests, and Amusement.

The situation of the truthful have turn out to be "The World of Tomorrow", and every of these specific zones displayed what the destiny could probable appear to be in every respective subject. For instance, inside the Transportation Zone, General Motors showed off a model metropolis designed for motors with super-highways from coast to coast and no purple lights. Ford displayed some of their maximum modern-day vehicle designs.

In different reveals, sincere attendees received a glimpse of television for the primary time. Color photos changed into moreover on display for all to look. General Electric delivered the arena to the fluorescent mild bulb, and one auditorium become prepared with any other new invention, air conditioning.

Westinghouse supplied the seven foot tall "Electro the Moto-Man". This grow to be a robot that could speak and carry out extraordinary duties. Meanwhile, in the Communications Zone, AT&T have turn out to be showing off a mechanized, synthetic voice that could talk to fairgoers. IBM had new gadgets in their private, together with the electric typewriter and an electric powered calculator.

Aside from the numerous famous, there were moreover stay indicates offering dancers and specific varieties of enjoyment. The Amusement Zone provided a whole lot of rides just like the ones placed at festivals in nowadays's worldwide. One of the maximum well-known rides changed into the parachute leap, which allowed human beings to revel in the exhilaration of dropping from a parachute.

Each day, the mayor of New York City, Fiorello La Guardia, might roam the grounds and greet fairgoers or entertain movie famous individual website online traffic. Franklin Roosevelt visited the sincere on its starting day or maybe formally "opened" the occasion. King George VI and Queen Elizabeth of England additionally visited the sincere.

The New York World's Fair changed into extremely famous. On its first day, almost hundred,000 human beings paid to go into the gates. By the give up of the honest's life in 1940, greater than 40 four million people had visited the "World of Tomorrow".

Chapter 13: When It All Came Crashing Down

Every decade has an event that looks to define it. Most could agree, for example, that the early 2000s were in large aspect described via the 9-11 terror assaults. Judging from how an entire lot blood and treasure became spilled within the warfare on terror that ran rampant in some unspecified time in the future of these years, this appears nearly beyond dispute. And now that we are in the 2020s, it seems pretty clear that this decade can be dictated with the resource of using the devastating outbreak of COVID-19. Most might also agree that this one viral outbreak has affected and disrupted every thing of our lives, and specialists say this can keep for some time.

Just as the ones a long term have their definitive issues, so too, did the Nineteen Thirties—and that topic modified into the Great Depression. But as with COVID-19, the occasion that kicked all of it off happened the previous one year. At the tail prevent of the Roaring Twenties, the stock marketplace took a precipitous dive.

The Twenties saw what specialists now say come to be an unprecedented amount of speculation within the inventory marketplace. In the ones days, the not unusual Joe (with out a bargain collateral to talk of), have become stepping into on the ground ground and putting bids. Everything seemed great. But then, on October 24, 1929, some factor came about. The stock began out to fall.

In response, some of the buyers who have been looking for at the reasonably-priced, with so-called margin investments (stocks sold with borrowed coins) were compelled to promote off all at once so as to interrupt even. This turn out to be now not quality horrible records for the man or woman investor, but additionally the banks that have been backing the stocks that have been supplied on this credit rating. This sudden loss brought about a downward spiral in which banks commenced to fail, and mortgages had been foreclosed upon.

President Herbert Hoover, meanwhile, didn't appear to take the problem too drastically. He assured the overall public that everything might probable blow over in handiest a couple of months and insisted that irrespective of the quick aberration of the inventory marketplace crash, the American financial device became "on a legitimate and rich basis." Numerous panicked Americans, inside the intervening time, had been emptying their savings money owed and thereby exacerbating the scenario even further. Known as a "financial institution run," the ones mad dashes for coins triggered the disintegrate of severa big banks. As the us of a slumped right right into a melancholy, countrywide layoffs have been rampant.

In moderate of the massive layoffs within the route of the COVID-19 disaster inside the spring and summer season of 2020, the area of new years can relate. But there's a huge difference amongst what passed off in contemporary information and what took place decrease back in 1929–30. During the lockdown added on through the usage of the Coronavirus in 2020, folks who've been compelled to stay at home and no longer art work were given government useful resource. Such matters had been not coming near close to underneath Hoover. On the other, he flat out refused to render lots beneficial aid in any respect to the unemployed. In Hoover's mind, an emergency stimulus might handiest feature a disincentive and encourage parents to live domestic and no longer paintings.

Hoover genuinely appeared to accept as true with that people needed to undergo a bit to recognize that they had to get available, bust their butts, and get a method – however there have been no jobs to get. And not like what took place in 2020 with the lockdown from COVID-19, there has been no moratorium on lease, loan, or software bills. After the crash of 1929, in case you misplaced your machine and couldn't pay hire, you have got got been evicted. If you couldn't pay your loan, you have got been foreclosed upon. If you couldn't pay your electric powered powered or gas invoice, it became near off.

There end up no protection internet, there has been no interest, and this become apparently what Hoover idea human beings wished that allows you to get inspired to artwork. But fast sufficient, even Hoover would possibly need to understand that it wasn't without a doubt that people have been being lazy and looking to appearance in advance to a handout. The problem was lots deeper than that, and as pillar after pillar of the financial gadget crumbled, for the not unusual person there has been honestly no gainful employment to be discovered.

Another problem affecting America's economy that could in turn come to have an effect on the entire worldwide modified into a touch something known as the "Hawley-Smoot Tariff." This one piece of guidelines significantly exacerbated the state of affairs via the usage of way of growing import charge lists thru forty% to 48%. The rate lists had a dramatic impact on agricultural imports, elevating the costs in grocery stores and kicking off a change battle with numerous countries.

Hoover absolutely finished the fee lists so that you can shore up help for the American farmer, however when coupled with the instability already inside the monetary system after the stock market crash, this proved to be a recipe for catastrophe. It had a domino impact at the region monetary device due to the truth as import fees had been raised, Americans grew to grow to be inward and stopped trying to find goods from remote places.

This then delivered on a stress on several European economies that have been despite the truth that obtaining higher from the effects of the First World War. Germany, specifically, became in fact suffering. Germany become already having to pay harsh reparations for its thing in the battle, and having its exports curtailed on this fashion proved to be sincerely devastating. As Germany determined itself unable to beautify its lagging monetary device, Germans tried to find out a way spherical a number of the pressure they were underneath with the beneficial resource of making a "customs union" with the kingdom of Austria in 1931.

Chapter 14: Hoover Fails And Roosevelt Takes Over

By most debts, President Herbert Hoover didn't take the signs of the imminent Great Depression very drastically, however in December of 1931, he shaped the Reconstruction Finance Corporation (or RFC for quick). Finally, there can be some government aid – however this useful resource changed into geared toward huge agencies, now not the commonplace American.

The RFC become more frequently than not supposed to provide a bailout for railroads, banks, and unique vital industries. The common citizens, within the intervening time, have been left in big factor unemployed and in loads of instances without even a roof over their heads. As mother and father had been evicted from homes thru landlords or had their homes foreclosed upon via the use of banks, they had been regularly pressured to create makeshift tent corporations. In the bitterly sarcastic mood of the times, such shantytowns have become known as "Hooverville."

Although no longer all the blame for the crumble may be located on President Hoover, he changed into the president on the time of the disaster, so American residents glaringly regarded in the direction of him for management. They moreover couldn't assist however consider that when Hoover grow to be first elected, he had promised a life of ease beneath his presidency. His notorious slogan throughout the 1928 presidential campaign, anyhow, became that there might be "a hen in every pot and a automobile in every storage."

In 1932, famed socialist author and rabble-rouser, Oscar Ameringer, need to seem in advance than a very specific taking note of completed with the useful resource of way of the House and proportion testimony about the dire straits of those he encountered on the street sooner or later of the early days of the Great Depression. At one element he described selecting up some hitchhikers. "I picked up a circle of relatives. The lady modified into hugging a vain chook below a ragged coat. When I requested her wherein she had procured the chicken, first she knowledgeable me that she discovered it useless in the road, after which brought in grim humor, 'They promised me a bird in the pot, and now I had been given mine.'"[1]

Besides the political dig at Herbert Hoover's pledge, it became truely a few as an possibility dark humor for a person to openly admit to scavenging roadkill for his or her dinner. But whilst people didn't apprehend wherein their next meal might come from, they did some component they'll to stay on. As is the case in dire times, pleasure need to go out the window as regards to survival.

It modified right into a commonplace scene to discover humans recognition round outdoor eating places before they closed, hoping for some leftovers. If they acquired none, some determined souls may additionally even inn to going through the garbage to find out food.

Yet notwithstanding the troubles that the not unusual American grow to be faced with, Hoover modified into reluctant to render any shape of governmental useful resource to person Americans. Furthermore, he continued to keep in mind that any sources that have been expended with the useful resource of the federal authorities must trickle down from the top. He idea that if government helped those on top of big organisation, they could in turn help the American citizens through growing jobs to appoint them.

As the 1932 presidential election drew near, but, even Hoover needed to admit that his efforts at trickle-down economics were no longer running. The destitute American humans needed jobs and that they desired them now. For this cause, he shifted gears and began to create federally sanctioned advent duties, hoping to put a big phase of the overall public lower again to art work. But for max, the efforts appeared to be too little, too overdue.

Meanwhile, Hoover's challenger in the imminent presidential election, democratic candidate Franklin Delano Roosevelt, preached a message of the usage of the general power of the federal government to raise the commonplace American up. Roosevelt were a governor of New York – the epicenter of the stock marketplace crash – and he knew complete well how a bargain the common citizen were ravaged through the use of the fallout of this disaster.

Franklin Delano Roosevelt knew that Americans weren't without a doubt being lazy, as Hoover so frequently seemed to insinuate; he knew that they might art work inside the event that they were definitely given the method to reap this. While he didn't continuously make it easy exactly how he became going to do it, Roosevelt proclaimed that if the people made him president, he might also make certain that everyone were given a sincere shake and promised a "new deal" for "the forgotten guy."

Roosevelt, at this point in his lifestyles, may want to sympathize pretty well with the lousy, inclined, and forgotten. He struck a resonant chord and consequently beat Hoover without hassle at the poll container. Even despite the fact that he come to be a person born into affluence, in the 1920s, Roosevelt confronted a reckoning that made him re-study the whole thing: he have been with polio. The disorder had ravaged his frame and had rendered him no longer capable of observe his legs.

Although in later years he constantly stood up with leg braces to talk at a podium, unbeknownst to most of the overall public, he is probably in a wheelchair for lots of the relaxation of his existence. Roosevelt got here to in my opinion apprehend what it grow to be want to need assist, and so his enlightened perspectives may want to come to form his very own efforts to render aid to individuals who had been struggling within the wake of the Great Depression.

He most actually had his paintings reduce out for him, but, and by the time Roosevelt become sworn into place of work in March of 1933, the unemployment rate changed into at a whopping 25%. Also, because of a loss of demand, business agency output changed into manner down and farmers within the agricultural area located themselves having to (really) burn up their harvests, thinking about that that that they had no one to shop for the extra.

But the most essential trouble changed into the banks. In the panic after the inventory marketplace crash, many financial establishments suffered from "financial organisation runs" wherein panicked clients withdrew all their cash all of sudden, inflicting the banks to disintegrate. This have come to be the number one hassle that President Roosevelt needed to address upon taking place of work. In an attempt to perform that, he declared a "countrywide banking tour" actually a couple of days after turning into president, and had all of the banks close to.

Despite how carefree all of this can sound, it become now not certainly a method of giving beleaguered bankers a destroy; it have become a top-down method to shutting down a failing financial gadget just so critical maintenance might be made. President Roosevelt have grow to be doing the very detail that his predecessor Hoover have been loath to do; he became the use of the power of the federal authorities to dictate to the banks truly how they need to get decrease lower back into enterprise.

Shortly thereafter, Roosevelt signed the Emergency Banking Act into law, which enabled the Federal Reserve to offer coins to banks which have been floundering simply so they may come once more on line and serve folks who depended on them with their cash. This become something exceptional at a few stage inside the Hoover administration, which never might also need to have conceived of dipping into reserve cash to hold struggling banks afloat.

The treasury department, alongside side meting out useful aid, moreover took on an lively function in inspecting and certifying the solvency of banks in advance than they opened their doorways to clients. This caused the established order of the Federal Deposit Insurance Corporation, or FDIC for short. This is the organization that maintains to make certain human beings these days that when they positioned their cash into a monetary organization, it's going to nonetheless be there the next day, because it's FDIC-insured.

After the banking excursion, President Roosevelt have end up capable to persuade the overall public that they might be better off taking the coins they had stashed in their houses out from under beds, and out of cookie jars, and setting it lower back into those federally-backed financial institution money owed. It emerge as useful that during comparison to President Hoover, President Roosevelt turned into a fantastic communicator and changed into able to deliver an cause in the back of subjects in a manner that the commonplace citizen need to recognize. Roosevelt was able to make the reference to people as to why doing what he asked of them become so vital. He made it easy to people who listened to him that not nice would possibly their cash be secure, however by using setting their cash all over again into the banks, they could be able to assist him restart the financial machine. Americans listened to Roosevelt and heeded his recommendation, and the very subsequent day humans have been out in droves setting their cash once more into the banks.

Getting the banks lower back on-line have turn out to be step one in Franklin Delano Roosevelt's plan for restoration, and it had lengthy long gone an entire lot better than all of us had anticipated. But he and the nation although had an extended road earlier of them. Roosevelt had discovered out loads in reality with the aid of listening to all President Herbert Hoover's mistakes. He now had his personal specific plan for recovery, and most effective time may additionally tell if it might art work.

Chapter 15: Getting Americans Back To Work

For hardworking Americans who've been used to identifying themselves thru their career, the dearth in their jobs changed into no longer simplest a lack of income, however a loss of their very identification. In cities for the duration of the u . S ., scores of despairing unemployed roamed the streets searching for art work. Former criminal professionals, doctors, bricklayers, carpenters, and so forth every went via the motions of lifestyles, but with out an outlet for his or her respective vocations, they felt hopeless and decided.

Roosevelt sought to get humans once more on the assignment in 3 levels that consisted of consolation, recuperation, and reform. First, he may do all he might also need to to alleviate individuals who've been in dire monetary straits, he may also then attention on convalescing the elements of the economic system that might be salvaged, and ultimately, he may want to trouble a reformation of the monetary gadget designed to defend against future monetary disturbance.

Early in Roosevelt's presidency he created a modern-day-day application geared closer to getting human beings lower returned to art work. It have become referred to as the Civilian Conservation Corps, and it employed the unemployed in droves for special, federally sanctioned projects in introduction and huge landscaping efforts together with draining swamplands and searching after countrywide parks. This software by the use of and massive employed young men and grow to be so whole that precise dormitories have been even created for the human beings. This allowed humans to be picked up proper off the street (actually) – and no longer handiest were they given a hobby however even an area to stay whilst doing it.

Another important jobs software program that changed into created rapid thereafter grow to be the WPA, or Works Progress Administration. This may add even extra jobs and will in time end up the middle-piece of Roosevelt's recovery software to get the dominion out of the Great Depression.

Those who labored for the WPA labored on a full-size style of fundamental tasks which consist of building roads, airports, schools, or maybe absolutely bizarre jobs which encompass the recovery of vintage library books. It became a piece of a trial-and-mistakes method to look what might in all likelihood work and what did now not, but the WPA actively supported challenge introduction in all bureaucracy with a view to get an keen citizenry another time to work.

The WPA also superior ladies's rights specially, due to the truth for one of the first times in the nation's facts, those jobs from the federal authorities paid every men and women on the same price. The WPA could in all likelihood stay in pressure until 1943, and in the direction of that point, countless Americans of all backgrounds might get hold of gainful and good sized employment.

As a great deal because the WPA focused on huge industry jobs, it additionally created programs for creatives like musicians, actors, artists, and writers. Unemployed journalists, as an example, had been given jobs writing down local people recollections and bills of existence in faraway sections of the kingdom for diverse anthology tasks sanctioned by using the federal government. Much of our documentation of the Great Depression itself can be attributed to these efforts.

Writers have been also given jobs to write down adventure courses about severa areas of the united states. Actors who've been struggling considering Hollywood closed its doors on them had been all at once being employed to perform government-supported theatrical dramas. It became the WPA that still gave upward thrust to the FAP (Federal Art Project) which provided an outlet for artists, letting them churn out over 225,000 portions of artwork to be enjoyed thru the overall public.

Unlike Hoover, who believed that it become the challenge of right-hearted buddies, church buildings, and charity organizations to assist individuals who had fallen on hard times, President Roosevelt created the closing safety net when he signed social safety into regulation in 1935.

Another wonderful boon established spherical this time have emerge as that of the National Labor Relations Act. This act labored to promote collective bargaining among employers and personnel.

Chapter 16: Utilizing A Bit Of American Ingenuity And Knowhow

A Nineteen Thirties airship, furthermore referred to as a blimp

Before massive authorities assist packages had been underway, the commonplace American have become already looking to make do the outstanding they'll. They say that necessity is the mother of invention, and it changed into out of determined necessity that many Americans have become so inventive in how they went approximately their lives in the course of the Great Depression. For one detail, while cash wasn't available, human beings fell over again at the historic way of life of bartering.

Many human beings for the duration of this period had their non-public gardens and outside chickens. But in hard times, those requirements had been used as a form of foreign cash. If one own family needed a few thing, they could frequently trade with a few distinctive for diverse forms of produce or domestic-crafted items. This bartering tool changed into used a protracted manner and huge. A medical medical doctor is probably paid for his offerings to rural patients with luggage of potatoes or onions, for instance.

Music—in particular Jazz tune—became all of the rage. Americans with plenty of downtime have been sitting across the radio and actively listening to this new and interesting paintings form.

The radio moreover became a device of the U.S. Government with the commonplace incidence of President Roosevelt's fireplace chats being achieved thru the medium. During these exchanges, Roosevelt have become capable to talk to the American people immediately in his informal and charismatic manner, teaching them in as smooth terms as viable about the improvement being made and what despite the fact that needed to be completed.

But FDR wasn't the best one the use of the strength of the radio, for it end up round this time that a well-known priest known as Father Coughlin started to address the kingdom on his own radio show. This priest normally mentioned politics masses greater than he stated faith and he have become a regular commentator at the country of the Great Depression. Initially, Coughlin, who've emerge as a critic of Hoover, supported Franklin Roosevelt's efforts, but fast he became critical. Coughlin called Franklin a liar and criticized a number of his social applications as being not something brief of socialism.

Another of FDR's incredible warring parties modified into a hint-stated senator from Louisiana, Huey Long. He seemed to be championing socialist doctrine outright. He mentioned curbing the profits of the rich at the same time as organising a essential annual profits of $2500 for the not unusual American, in addition to particular presents for housing and education.

Huey Long emerge as a populist who may want to initiate the going for walks beauty, the very people whose cooperation Roosevelt depended upon. Long very well have to have supplied a splendid challenge to Roosevelt, but his efforts to decrease FDR and his New Deal got here to an abrupt end on September 8th, 1935, whilst Long changed into reduce down through an murderer's bullet.

Surprisingly, the aforementioned Father Coughlin was clearly a supporter of Long's. This seems as an alternative bizarre for the motive that Coughlin railed towards the evils of socialism and lots of Long's proposed regulations were an awful lot more socialist in nature than Roosevelt's. But at any rate, as fast as Long have emerge as killed, Coughlin have emerge as even greater radical. Coughlin started out to openly rail within the course of FDR's management or even extra alarmingly, made outrageous claims that the New Deal have grow to be a part of a Jewish conspiracy, or as he referred to as it, the artwork of "coins changers."

As Coughlin have grow to be increasingly more of a capture 22 state of affairs to Roosevelt's recuperation efforts at some degree inside the Great Depression, FDR enlisted the beneficial useful resource of a person who knew Father Coughlin properly—Joseph P. Kennedy. Joe Kennedy modified into the daddy of future President John F. Kennedy and modified into the U.S. Ambassador to the UK on the time. He became a rising big name within the Democratic birthday celebration. Joe have become additionally a Roman Catholic who come to be on intimate terms with Coughlin.

Roosevelt made it Joe Kennedy's procedure to muzzle the preacher and he did so thru coordinating with one in every of a type Catholic notables together with Bishop Francis Spellman and the destiny Pope Pius XII, Cardinal Eugenio Pacelli. Through them, he managed to get the Vatican to reserve Coughlin to stop and desist. Coughlin though criticized Roosevelt whilst he also can need to, portray his efforts inside the course of restoration from the Depression as socialism at high-quality and communism at worst.

The average American, inside the meantime, was living a greater communal existence, with prolonged family or even pals all living collectively in tighter and tighter regions. In the cities, houses had been often cramped and crowded, and because of a rise in residence fees inside the 1930s, only a few have been inside the marketplace to buy.

For the ones who've been owners, this hard duration found advances in home home device with things like fridges, washing machines, and clothes dryers, however maximum human beings absolutely couldn't offer you with the money for them. On the opportunity, in preference to adopting the most cutting-edge-day-day home system, most had to hotel to masses more old style manner on the same time because it came to washing clothes or storing their meals.

Most washed garments with the useful useful resource of hand after which hung them out to dry of their backyard. And in preference to using a refrigerator, things which include root cellars were pretty commonplace locations to keep their food. These matters have been specially vital if the strength end up lessen off, thinking about that those antique fashion strategies of residing did not require energy.

But because of the ones traumatic conditions, many new enhancements got here out of this period. We take a number of them as a proper nowadays, which incorporates nylon, which changed into used for making girls's stockings.

This have become moreover the very last decade wherein scotch tape grow to be invented. Many a Depression-technology jobseeker wore out the soles in their footwear and needed to motel to this tape an fantastic manner to hold them together! The Thirties moreover noticed extra extravagant experiments with airships, which incorporates an instance wherein a huge airship turned into used to select up postal parcels, ushering in a very particular transport habitual of "air mail."

The improvements of the Thirties were frequently sensible however absolutely innovative in scope. They used the cutting-edge-day generation an amazing way to make existence a touch bit less difficult. The time of the Great Depression turned into tough, however a bit American ingenuity and knowhow went an prolonged manner within the course of making topics higher.

Chapter 17: The Dirty 1930s: Fighting Back Against The Dust Bowl

Since the nineteenth century, the states of the terrific plains inclusive of Colorado, Kansas, New Mexico, Oklahoma, and Texas had been an area of large farming. Hopeful Americans had poured into this area from the east with a desire to domesticate the huge swaths of grassland. They had been pretty successful and shortly the plains had been sincerely included in farms.

This, however, created an sudden environmental calamity. The natural grasses of the plains have prolonged, thick roots that keep them firmly imbedded deep inside the dirt. These deep roots set up what is referred to as a "sod mat," that's able to keeping moisture for lengthy intervals and furthermore prevents disruption to the topsoil from wind.

But the grasslands were modified thru farms with vegetation which includes corn, wheat, and oats – which amplify plenty within the direction of the floor. Now the wind need to blow the looser topsoil round in dusty maelstroms, whilst the herbal grass could have better secured the dust.

The problem certainly began, however, when the plains vicinity have become struck with a extreme drought. The severity of the drought supposed that the grassless soil, which grow to be already no longer nicely geared up to maintain moisture, have come to be lots dryer and consequently even greater without troubles picked up via the wind.

Making subjects even worse, the ones dry situations proved to be the best breeding floor for locusts due to the fact those pests love to location their eggs in dry, sandy soil. So it turned into that the beleaguered farmers of the Thirties were confronted with biblical-fashion plagues of drought, dirt storms, and locusts. The locusts really have been given so terrible that now not handiest did they eat up all the vegetation, they clearly destroyed farming tools, and in a few times fed on the very paint off of the homesteads.

But the worst a part of this period turned into, of route, the huge dust storms themselves. On May eleven, 1934, some 350 tons of dust moved throughout the plains unexpectedly in a single big typhoon. But one of the worst and maximum memorable storms passed off on April 14, 1935, in an occasion that modified into later known as "Black Sunday." On within the period in-between, a dirt typhoon stated to were one thousand miles huge swept over the plains, moving approximately 1500 miles in simplest days' time.

It grow to be clearly miserable for folks who lived beneath the ones situations. Even despite the fact that human beings locked themselves inner their houses with the doorways and domestic windows close to, whilst the dust storm got here, the dirt may seem to seep via the very partitions, leaving humans with dust on their faces, in their hair—and extra alarmingly, of their lungs.

Dust storms posed a totally real health threat to those who lived on the plains and times of silicosis skyrocketed. Silicosis is a situation in which an accumulation of dust particles inside the lungs has destroyed the cilia, essentially shredding the lungs and making it tough for

Chapter 18: The Great Depression And The Rise Of Organized Crime

Although incredible within the Great Depression, organized crime honestly had its roots within the prohibition era of the Twenties. When alcohol changed into made illegal in the United States, speakeasies popped up on many corners and maximum of them simply so came about to be on the payroll of organized crime. Besides presenting illicit liquor from bootleggers, the mob paid off police and distinct officers to ensure that the joints they "protected" weren't scenario to any midnight raids.

Even on the identical time as FDR repealed prohibition, making alcoholic consumption prison yet again, prepared crime had grown so ubiquitous that they weren't going away on every occasion soon. They truly varied their sports sports. And with such pretty some unemployed they may typically find out determined souls who, now not able to earn a first rate living, commenced to hotel to incomes an indecent residing underneath the auspices of a criminal offense boss.

It probable didn't assist subjects that Hollywood regularly glorified those sports via the production of gangster flicks which consist of The Public Enemy and Little Caesar, which made the ones criminal syndicates out to be present day-day-day Robin Hoods who have been sincerely doing their awesome to make it at some level within the economic downturn.

Arguably the maximum notorious gangster, Chicago's Al Capone, had been locked up for tax evasion for the purpose that 1931. But it modified into after Capone changed into locked up that the real upward thrust of prepared crime began below mafiosos like

New York's Lucky Luciano. Although the Mafia couldn't make coins from alcohol sales after the repeal of prohibition, they quick crafted a useful illicit exchange which encompass playing, prostitution, and labor racketeering.

Indeed, the Mafia controlled to pc virus its manner into exertions unions if you want to glean cash via manner of the usage of bribing corporations, even at the same time as providing themselves as valid businessmen. Not best that, they frequently cultivated public agree with – even admiration – thru donating cash to charities along with soup kitchens. Such matters served to decorate the myth that the mob had the fantastic hobbies of the commonplace guy at coronary coronary heart.

And the east coast, big-town gangsters weren't the handiest situation. While the mob hid under the façade of legitimate enterprise, exceptional outlaws had been running amok, robbing banks left and right. These outlaw-fashion gangsters ran rampant in the Midwest and western states. These had been typically no longer related to criminal syndicates which include the Mafia and in the event that they have been, notable loosely so. Unbeholden to the big town crime bosses, these outlaws lived thru their very own phrases. These blanketed notorious crooks which includes John Dillinger, Machine Gun Kelly, Pretty Boy Floyd, and Bonnie and Clyde, who used rapid motors to rob banks left and proper all in the course of the u . S ..

These gangsters have been similar to the outlaws of the antique west who may additionally need to rob trains and banks inside the 19th century. Outlaws like Billy the Kid would possibly ride a horse right as lots as a teach and speak to for coins, and then experience off inside the opposite route. These instances of literal "toll road theft" are what added approximately such notoriety. The number one difference some of the outlaw gangsters of the 1800s and the 1930s, but, turn out to be that they used vehicles to make their getaway and toted machine guns as opposed to shotguns.

The poverty of the Great Depression helped to spawn this new breed of outlaws, as many that may not have been able to find a legitimate manner of earnings began out to show to crime as an alternative. During the Great Depression there has been a lack of remember in the banks, even after the FDIC did its terrific to guarantee buyers their money changed into steady – but the FDIC couldn't stop bank robberies.

As a string of heists passed off everywhere in the the united states, many started out out to lose faith in the competence of the police. Local police were commonly ill-equipped to deal with the ones carefully armed bandits – and those who have been courageous sufficient to rise as much as them were normally grow to be swiss cheese as those cold-blooded killers crammed them with lead. The policeman's popular revolver, in any case, become hardly ever a healthy for monetary agency robbers with gadget guns.

But things have been approximately to exchange. During the Thirties, FBI Director J. Edgar Hoover led the rate to area a forestall to this criminal hobby as speedy as and for all. He modified into in massive element a hit. Due to a huge mobilization of the FBI, with the useful useful resource of 1935 nearly all the notorious outlaw gangsters have been killed or placed inside the decrease back of bars.

The actual key to this fulfillment changed into the reality that with the useful resource of the mid-Nineteen Thirties, new regulation allowed the FBI to go u.S.A. Of america traces to pursue those crooks. Before this, crime was treated on a state-with the aid of-state foundation. This intended that within the past, all someone like John Dillinger needed to do grow to be go a country line and he might be stable. He should rob a financial group in Chicago, as an example, and then actually hurry on over to northern Indiana at the same time as his pursuers stopped at the nation line. Once the FBI had jurisdiction to move united states of america strains, it emerge as all but over for those outlaws.

Further tightening the noose turned into the implementation of substantial fingerprinting. It is stated that by manner of 1932, the FBI had over one hundred,000 fingerprints on file, and with the aid of the usage of 1946, that variety might also leap to one hundred million. Since it have become now stylish system to get the fingerprints of every accused person being processed, there was now a protracted-lasting file to be had even as repeat offenders were arrested all once more, in a while down the street.

It have become because of this that John Dillinger famously paid an underworld medical doctor (sure, crooks once in a while have their private shady private physicians) to modify his fingerprints. He installation an appointment with a German-American plastic fitness care professional by means of using the call of Wilhelm Loeser. Dr. Loeser reduce away the floor layers of Dillinger's palms in advance than subjecting them to hydrochloric acid.

It took some days for Dillinger's hands to heal, but as quickly as he healed up, his prints were in reality substantially altered. The great problem changed into that he now had the maximum precise and recognizable set of fingerprints within the world! Just consider it. What have become greater recognizable: his antique current set of prints, or the bizarrely mangled, warped, and distorted prints he have been given from soaking his fingertips in hydrochloric acid?

Chapter 19: The Lead-As Tons As World War Ii

Many have argued that the Great Depression didn't absolutely give up till World War II, for it modified into the Second World War that exceptionally ramped up production for the struggle try. Even even though America did no longer input the battle until 1941, thru 1939 American factories have been buzzing with exertions so that it will create tool for Britain and France who were duking it out with Germany because of the reality 1939.

The Great Depression helped to spark World War II. In order to hint the path that led there, one has to move returned to the prevent of World War I. We have stated that after the give up of the First World War,

Germany changed into left with an massive bill for reparations. Germany changed into already in ruin after the battle, and now became forced to pay out coins to the victors of the battle.

As the economic state of affairs worsened, it laid the seeds for discontent that could supply upward push to unstable, fascist leaders. Germany become a large number via the early Nineteen Thirties, and proper at some point of the time FDR became elected president in 1933, Adolf Hitler rose to energy. While FDR end up making sweeping modifications to America with packages just like the WPA, Hitler, too, changed into given a superb amount of authority over the German state. At a time at the same time as maximum Germans had lost preference, Hitler supplied himself as a savior decide – rapid sufficient, however, he ought to lead they all to ruin.

Hitler controlled to mobilize Germany's flagging enterprise and create jobs for the human beings through infrastructure, and extra ominously, through armaments. As Germany constructed up its capability to earnings war, it commenced out pushing to gain territory that it felt it had out of place, or that otherwise rightfully belonged to them. This caused a push into the Rhineland in 1936, the seizure of the Sudetenland, and the annexation of Austria.

Britain, which stood because of the truth the number one European us of a, tried to assuage the Germans in these acquisitions, questioning it better to offer in than to spark every other war. But at the same time as Germany driven its good fortune and invaded Poland in 1939, the Brits had in the end had sufficient and declared struggle on Germany. France also declared struggle at the Germans and will short end up their maximum important goal. Germany might probable launch a vicious blitzkrieg into France in 1940, cute the location with how rapid German tanks have to capture French territory.

Even extra disturbing, a few Americans even sympathized with Nazi Germany. America had a huge populace of German-Americans on the time, some quality a generation or eliminated from their ancestral place of origin. These sympathizers ranged from the ones who've been simply quietly supportive to the more sinister, all-out Nazi sympathizers. The most famous of those modified into the so-known as German American Bund.

The German American Bund consisted of American citizens who have been seasoned-Nazi. This institution may additionally need to quick be a pinnacle aim of the "House Committee on Un-American Activities" and the chief of the Bund might be arrested and in the long run deported. But dispositions in Germany were now not the most effective international happenings that have been turning into worrisome to the us.

Even at the same time as Germany changed into bulldozing through Europe, Japan changed into waging a brutal conflict with

China and driving American hobbies out. Although neither Japan nor America desired conflict in the Nineteen Thirties, Japan's militancy in the place became already pushing the two international places to the threshold. In December of 1937, a complete four years earlier than Pearl Harbor, the Japanese sank the Panay, an American navy craft that became stationed in China's Yangtze River.

Japan changed into not however equipped to evoke the sleeping huge of American reprisal, and in the long run apologized and doled out cash to the patients. Yet at the same time, the Japanese broaden endured to bother American installations which consist of American-run hospitals and missions, regularly pushing U.S. Affect out of China. Even even though no person favored to admit it, many in the U.S. Authorities knew that a battle with Japan changed into all however inevitable. And as such, efforts have been made to make certain that the U.S. Navy may be effectively mobilized in each the Atlantic and the Pacific.

As the last decade drew to a near, within the period in-between, Roosevelt have become undertaking the save you of his 2nd term in office. Up until that point, no U.S. President had lengthy beyond beyond terms. To be easy, there was not but a regulation mandating a -time period limit, however with the aid of sheer example, going all the manner decrease returned to George Washington, every American president had stepped down after their second term.

Franklin Delano Roosevelt changed into the primary who dared to buck this fashion, and in 1940 ran for a 3rd time period. He ran toward the Republican candidate Wendell L. Wilkie, someone who had challenged some of Roosevelt's rules within the past. Roosevelt charted a consistent course at a few stage within the election, however, and by the usage of way of November of 1940 he effects obtained himself a third time period in place of job.

France, inside the meantime, had already fallen to the Nazis, and England have turn out to be in an ever more precarious function. It come to be consequently vital in Roosevelt's 0.33 term for the Americans to render as heaps resource to England as possible. Roosevelt knew that if England emerge as knocked out of the conflict, Germany is probably an lousy lot extra tough to forestall. Roosevelt knew that American protection relied on British protection, and so he recommitted himself to assisting Britain (and later, different allies) as lots as he must. He did so with the "Lend-Lease Act" which have become exceeded on March 11, 1941.

With the lend-rent, the U.S. (regardless of the reality that officially independent inside the struggle at this difficulty), agreed to fabricate and deliver critical tool to Britain. But as masses as this useful resource proved important in retaining Britain alive in the fight in the route of Nazi Germany, the lend-lease software program helped America extra than some element else – it changed into the huge demand for American gadgets that invigorated the American monetary system.

With the modern demand for employees in the factories, the unemployment charge inside the United States went down dramatically. Instead of repute in line at a soup kitchen, parents have been suddenly repute in line to gain gainful employment at commercial organization factories anywhere in the country. During the Depression, no man or woman have to find out artwork however as soon because the conflict commenced out, due to immoderate call for, there has been a activity ready, quite certainly, on each nook.

Initially, the public, cautious of battle and foreign places entanglements, became quite skeptical of assisting the allied powers, however Roosevelt, alongside alongside together with his ordinary attraction and air of mystery, have become capable of slowly persuade the American public of the want. Again, he reached many humans through the use of radio. In his regular hearth chats, he grow to be capable of slowly get Americans used to the idea that they may need to do more for the conflict attempt.

The exciting issue about the lend-lease is that maximum of the countries that the U.S. Lent its beneficial useful resource to didn't precisely pay America lower lower back. So wherein inside the worldwide did the U.S. Authorities get the coins for all of this large manufacturing? They raised it thru conflict bonds. Yes, thru mainly instituted government bonds, nearly $185.7 million might in the end be raised. During all of this fundraising America modified into slowly drifting nearer and nearer toward playing an active detail in the battle.

This destiny must then be sealed on December 7, 1941, while Japan launched a sneak assault at the American naval base at

Pearl Harbor in Hawaii. President Roosevelt pledged revenge in competition to the "dastardly assault" via the Empire of Japan, and the united states could thereafter be absolutely engaged in World War II.

Now that the U.S. Was formally at struggle, not only have become enterprise churning for the battle strive, however younger humans have been being drafted into the armed offerings to combat the battle in individual. In all, approximately 15 million ladies and men would leave civilian life to take part inside the military straight away. With every the factories and the military rapidly filling positions with American residents, by means of 1942 the unemployment price (which became around 20% whilst Roosevelt first took place of business), dropped proper all the way down to loads less than 5%. Despite the vital overhauls to the economic gadget at some stage in the FDR years, it seems pretty smooth that the catastrophe of the Great Depression maximum probable met its in shape in the path of the frenzied buildup and implementation of World War II.

www.ingramcontent.com/pod-product-compliance
Lightning Source LLC
Chambersburg PA
CBHW071441080526
44587CB00014B/1947